Statistical Language Models for Information Retrieval

Synthesis Lectures on Human Language Technologies

Editor
Graeme Hirst
University of Toronto

Synthesis Lectures on Human Language Technologies publishes monographs on topics relating to natural language processing, computational linguistics, information retrieval, and spoken language understanding. Emphasis is placed on important new techniques, on new applications, and on topics that combine two or more HLT subfields.

Statistical Language Models for Information Retrieval
ChengXiang Zhai
2009

Statistical Language Models for Information Retrieval
ChengXiang Zhai

ISBN: 978-3-031-01002-6   paperback
ISBN: 978-3-031-02130-5   ebook

DOI 10.1007/978-3-031-02130-5

A Publication in the Springer series
SYNTHESIS LECTURES ON ADVANCES IN AUTOMOTIVE TECHNOLOGY

Lecture #1
Series Editor: Graeme Hirst, University of Toronto

Series ISSN
Synthesis Lectures on Human Language Technologies
ISSN pending.

Statistical Language Models for Information Retrieval

ChengXiang Zhai

Department of Computer Science

Graduate School of Library and Information Science
Department of Statistics
Institute for Genomic Biology
University of Illinois at Urbana-Champaign

SYNTHESIS LECTURES ON HUMAN LANGUAGE TECHNOLOGIES #1

ABSTRACT

As online information grows dramatically, search engines such as Google are playing a more and more important role in our lives. Critical to all search engines is the problem of designing an effective retrieval model that can rank documents accurately for a given query. This has been a central research problem in information retrieval for several decades. In the past ten years, a new generation of retrieval models, often referred to as statistical language models, has been successfully applied to solve many different information retrieval problems. Compared with the traditional models such as the vector space model, these new models have a more sound statistical foundation and can leverage statistical estimation to optimize retrieval parameters. They can also be more easily adapted to model non-traditional and complex retrieval problems. Empirically, they tend to achieve comparable or better performance than a traditional model with less effort on parameter tuning.

This book systematically reviews the large body of literature on applying statistical language models to information retrieval with an emphasis on the underlying principles, empirically effective language models, and language models developed for non-traditional retrieval tasks. All the relevant literature has been synthesized to make it easy for a reader to digest the research progress achieved so far and see the frontier of research in this area. The book also offers practitioners an informative introduction to a set of practically useful language models that can effectively solve a variety of retrieval problems. No prior knowledge about information retrieval is required, but some basic knowledge about probability and statistics would be useful for fully digesting all the details.

KEYWORDS

Information retrieval, search engines, retrieval models, language models, smoothing, topic models.

To my wife Mei, my son Alex, and my parents.

Contents

Preface

Recent years have seen an explosive growth of online information. As the most useful tools for combating information overload, search engines are now becoming increasingly important and have been successfully deployed in many different application domains. The rapid rise of the search engine industry has generated much interest in information retrieval (IR) research and education. This book is designed to help meet the needs of researchers, students, and developers of search engine applications for learning about the frontier of information retrieval research, particularly recent progress in developing new information retrieval models.

Critical to all search engines is the problem of designing an effective retrieval model that can rank documents accurately for a given query. This has been a central research problem in information retrieval for several decades. In the past ten years, a new generation of retrieval models, often referred to as statistical language models, has been successfully applied to solve many different information retrieval problems. Compared with the traditional models such as the vector space model, these new models have many advantages, such as a sound statistical foundation, possibilities of leveraging available statistical estimation methods to optimize retrieval parameters, and easiness to adapt to non-traditional and complex retrieval problems.

The main purpose of this book is to review and synthesize the large body of literature on statistical language models for information retrieval so that a reader can easily digest the literature and see the frontier of research in this area. Emphasis has been put on covering the underlying principles of all the models, empirically effective language models, and language models developed for non-traditional retrieval tasks. A secondary goal of the book is to introduce to practitioners a set of practically useful language models that can effectively solve a variety of retrieval application problems.

The book is based on a series of tutorials on this topic that I have given at various information retrieval conferences, and is an expansion of a related survey that I wrote for the Foundations and Trends in Information Retrieval [17]. Compared with the survey, this book is more selfcontained and covers all the basic models with much more detail. The survey was written mainly for researchers with some previous knowledge about information retrieval, but the book is intended to be understandable to readers without prior background on information retrieval. To achieve this goal, the book has included a concise introduction to the basic concepts in information retrieval and an entire chapter to provide a general survey of all information retrieval models. It has also much more detailed explanation of the basic models, which should help readers with no background in information retrieval to digest the materials. Unfortunately, given the size of the book, it is hard to include all the necessary background materials. Thus, in cases when some discussions are not easy to follow due to unfamiliarity with some concepts in information retrieval, the readers should refer to some textbooks on information retrieval (e.g., [18], [19], [20], and [21])). Although no prior knowledge about IR is assumed, most materials presented in the book rely on some basic knowledge of probability and statistics such as multinomial distribution and maximum likelihood estimation. Readers with no such knowledge are recommended to first read some textbook on probability and statistics (e.g., [22]) before reading this book. However, readers with no knowledge about probability and statistics should still be able to understand all the major ideas and follow most of the high-level discussions.

The organization of the book is as follows. The first chapter provides some background on information retrieval and statistical language models for readers with no such background. Chapter 2 contains a broad overview of different retrieval models to give the readers a big picture about the entire space of retrieval models and where language models fit in. Starting from Chapter 3, we then systematically introduce various kinds of retrieval models based on language modeling. In Chapter 3, we introduce the very first generation of language models (called simple query likelihood retrieval models) which are computationally as efficient as any existing retrieval model. Their good empirical performance has motivated many follow-up studies and extensions of language models for retrieval. In Chapter 4, we discuss a large body of work all aiming at extending and improving the basic language modeling approach. These models (called complex query likelihood retrieval models) may achieve better performance, but also tend to be computationally much more expensive than the simple query likelihood retrieval models. Feedback is an important component in an IR system, but it turns out that there is some difficulty in supporting feedback with the query likelihood retrieval models. In Chapter 5, we present the Kullback-Leibler divergence retrieval model, which generalizes the query likelihood retrieval model and also accommodates feedback (particularly pseudo feedback) through using feedback information to improve the estimate of a query language model. These feedback models are among the most effective language models for retrieval. In Chapter 6, we further review a wide range of applications of language models to different special retrieval tasks where a standard language model is often extended or adapted to better fit a specific application. In Chapter 7, we introduce a family of language models that can be used to conduct latent topic analysis and discuss their applications in information retrieval. Finally, we summarize and discuss future research directions in Chapter 8.

The book can be used as a supplementary textbook for a graduate or undergraduate course on information retrieval or related topics (e.g., natural language processing, machine learning) to help students gain in-depth understanding of the basic language models for information retrieval. For advanced models, however, the book only provides a high level discussion, thus readers will still need to read the original papers to really understand them in detail. Chapters 2 and 7 are both relatively selfcontained, so they can be used as standing alone introductions to retrieval models and probabilistic topic models, respectively.

Many people have directly or indirectly contributed to the completion of this book, and I would like to thank all of them. First of all, I want to thank Graeme Hirst, editor of the Synthesis Lectures on Human Language Technologies series of the Synthesis Digital Library, and Michael Morgan, President of Morgan & Claypool Publishers, for offering me the opportunity to publish this book. They have also provided very useful feedback about the content of the book. I am very grateful to my Ph.D. advisor John Lafferty for his supervision of my dissertation on this topic; the main conceptual framework and a substantial part of this book are based on my dissertation. I am also very grateful to Jamie Callan for encouraging me to give a tutorial on this topic at several conferences. The tutorial has formed the basis of this book. Without John's technical advice and Jamie's encouragement, I would not have been able to write this book.

I gratefully acknowledge the support of my own research on this topic by the Advanced Research and Development Activity in Information Technology (ARDA) under its Statistical Language Modeling for Information Retrieval Research Program, by the National Science Foundation under a CAREER grant (IIS-0347933), by Google, Microsoft, and IBM through their research programs, and by the Alfred P. Sloan Foundation through a research fellowship. Any opinions, findings, and conclusions, or recommendations expressed in this book are, of course, those of the author and do not necessarily reflect the views of the sponsors.

I am greatly indebted to several people who have directly helped improving the quality of this book. Wessel Kraaij and another anonymous reviewer have carefully reviewed a draft of this book and offered extremely valuable comments which have helped to improve the quality of the book significantly. Donald Metzler and two other anonymous reviewers have provided many useful comments for the survey paper mentioned earlier; those comments have also helped improving the quality of this book. Naturally, any errors that remain are solely my own responsibility.

I also want to thank many researchers with whom I have had useful discussions on various topics covered in this book, especially my students and co-authors. Although I cannot list all the names here, I would like to mention W. Bruce Croft, Stephen Robertson, Victor Lavrenko, Rong Jin, Tao Tao, David A. Evans, Qiaozhu Mei, and Wessel Kraaij; all of them have influenced my understanding of some major technical issues discussed in the book.

Special thanks are due to C.L. Tondo and Sara Kreisman for their help with preparing the final version of the book.

Finally, and above all, I must thank my wife Mei for her love and huge support throughout the process of writing this book. I dedicate this book to her.

ChengXiang Zhai
Department of Computer Science

Graduate School of Library and Information Science
Department of Statistics
Institute for Genomic Biology
University of Illinois at Urbana-Champaign
January 2009

CHAPTER 1

Introduction

With the explosive growth of online information, such as news articles, email messages, scientific literature, government documents, and many other kinds of information on the Web, we are overwhelmed with huge amounts of information and have an urgent need for powerful software tools to help manage and make use of all the information. Search engines such as Google are by far the most useful tools to help combat information overload; their effectiveness directly affects our productivity and quality of life.

Information Retrieval (IR) is, in brief, the underlying science of search engines. As a research field, it is primarily concerned with developing theories, principles, algorithms, and systems to help a user find relevant information from a collection of text documents to satisfy some information need of the user. However, in a broader sense, IR is also concerned with many other tasks relevant to helping people manage and exploit information in general, such as text categorization, text clustering, text summarization, question answering, and information filtering. In this book, we primarily focus on search techniques, which are at the core of IR and are quite important for developing effective search engines. These techniques can also be very useful for many other tasks.

Research in IR can be dated back to the 1950's [3]. In early days, the primary applications were library systems and the users were mostly librarians. However, the recent growth of online information, especially the development of the Web, has enabled ordinary people to be the users of various search engines. Over the decades, IR researchers have developed a suite of search engine technologies, including indexing techniques, retrieval models, feedback techniques, user interfaces, and evaluation methodologies. These technologies have matured over time to enable many search engine applications, ranging from special-domain search engines such as PubMed (http://www.ncbi.nlm.nih.gov/pubmed/) through general Web search engines such as Google, Yahoo, and Live Search. Indeed, commercial IR systems have already been around for many years, and nowadays many IR toolkits are available for people to rapidly build a search engine application [4].

On the other hand, however, there are still many challenges to be solved in IR research. One of the most fundamental and important challenges is to develop a truly optimal retrieval model that is both effective and efficient and that can learn from feedback information over time. To understand this challenge, it is necessary to understand how a typical IR system works.

A main goal of any IR system is to rank documents optimally given a query so that highly relevant documents would be ranked above less relevant ones and nonrelevant ones. In order to achieve this goal, the system must be able to score documents so that a highly relevant document would tend to have a higher score than a nonrelevant one. Clearly, the retrieval accuracy of an IR system is directly determined by the quality of the scoring function adopted. Thus, not surprisingly, seeking an optimal scoring function (often called a retrieval function) has always been a major research challenge in information retrieval. A retrieval function is based on a retrieval model, which formally defines the notion of relevance and enables us to derive a retrieval function that can be computed to score and rank documents.

The search accuracy of an IR system is primarily determined by the soundness of its underlying retrieval model. Improvement of retrieval models would directly lead to improved utility of all search engine applications[1]. It is thus very important to understand which retrieval model is the best. The main purpose of this book is to introduce and review a family of promising new information retrieval models, all based on statistical modeling of natural language (i.e., statistical language models). Compared with traditional retrieval models (e.g., the vector-space model), these new approaches (often called language modeling approaches) perform equally well but have many advantages including sound statistical foundation, automatic setting of retrieval model parameter, and easily accommodating different retrieval tasks. The language modeling approaches have mostly been developed in the last ten years, yet, within this short period, they have already shown great promise for multiple retrieval tasks with very good empirical performance. Development of new language models is currently an active research area in information retrieval. It can thus be envisioned that the language modeling approaches will find more and more applications and may eventually replace the traditional retrieval models.

In the rest of this chapter, we will provide some background on both information retrieval and statistical language models to help readers who do not previously have such background to understand the rest of the book. Readers already familiar with information retrieval and language models can skip the rest of the chapter.

1.1   BASIC CONCEPTS IN INFORMATION RETRIEVAL

A basic information retrieval problem is set up as follows: We assume that there exists a *document collection* $C = \{D_1, ..., D_N\}$ where D_i is a text *document*. Given a *query* Q, the task of an information retrieval system is to return a ranked list of documents so that the documents ranked on the top are more relevant to the query than those ranked below them. In most studies, a document is assumed to be either relevant or nonrelevant (i.e., binary relevance). Although such a binary relevance assumption does not fully reflect the reality since relevance is a matter of degree, it makes it easier to collect user relevance judgments for evaluation. *Relevant documents* are what the user is looking for, and can be regarded as containing the expected answers to the query. Typically, ranking is done by first using a *retrieval function s* to score each document with respect to the query and then ranking all the documents based on their scores. That is, we have $s(Q, D_i) \in \Re$.

Typically, the query and documents are expressed in the same language, such as English, and both consist of a sequence of words in the language. Formally, let $V = \{w_1, ..., w_M\}$ be the *vocabulary* set of our language and w_i a word. We may denote a query as $Q = q_1, ..., q_m$ and a document as $D = d_1, ..., d_n$. In many retrieval models, the order of words in a query or a document

---

[1]Naturally, other components such as the user interface are also very important for an IR system.

is ignored, thus both Q and D would be a *bag of words*. Despite its simplicity, such a bag-of-words representation has been shown to perform quite well empirically; as a result, it remains the most popular representation used in virtually all the search engines.

However, such a representation would not be able to distinguish word sequences "street market" and "market street" which have quite different meanings. Thus, intuitively it is possible to improve retrieval accuracy by capturing the word order; unfortunately, as we will discuss later, it remains a major challenge to develop a robust retrieval model that can handle such word orders effectively in a general way. Most of our discussions in this book assume the bag-of-words representation.

As a computation problem, the retrieval problem is ill-defined because the quality of search results can only be judged by users of a retrieval system in a subjective way. Thus, in order to tell which retrieval method is the best, we must rely on users to make judgments or data sets created based on user judgments. The search results of a retrieval system are often evaluated in two ways: (1) conduct a user study where actual users would use the system and assess the quality of the search process and results; and (2) develop a gold standard test collection in advance and test a system using the test collection to assess the quality of search results.

The first way allows us to see the actual utility of a system, thus the evaluation results are more interpretable in terms of the usefulness of the system. However, due to the involvement of different users or the different status of the same user, it may be difficult to compare two systems reliably using this strategy. For example, if a user tries the same query on system A before trying it on system B, then by the time of trying system B, the user would have already become more familiar with the topic, which may cause bias in comparing the two systems. Another deficiency of the first way is the unavailability of many users to participate in the experiments.

Due to these reasons, the second way has been so far the most popular way of evaluating search results (especially in academia research). This evaluation methodology was developed by Cleverdon and colleagues in the 1960's [5], and is often called the *Cranfield evaluation method*. In this method, we would choose a sample collection of documents and a set of realistic queries (often from real users), and then have real users (ideally who designed the queries) to judge all the documents for each query to identify relevant documents. Binary relevance is assumed (i.e., a document is assumed to be either relevant or nonrelevant). The obtained *relevance judgments* can then be used to measure the accuracy of ranking (an ideal ranking would put all the relevant documents above all the nonrelevant ones).

In the early days of IR research, the document collections were small, and it was feasible to judge all the documents. As large document collections were used, it was no longer feasible to have human assessors to judge all the documents. Thus, a new strategy called "pooling" was proposed in [6]. The idea was to pool together all the top-ranked documents from a sufficiently large set of retrieval systems, and have human assessors to judge only this subset of documents for each query. When evaluating search results, we would assume all the unjudged documents are nonrelevant. Although the judgments are incomplete, we can hope that such judgments are sufficient to distinguish a good retrieval system from a poor one. This strategy has been adopted in many tasks of TREC, an annual conference for evaluation of text retrieval techniques (see http://trec.nist.gov/), and so far, it has been working well in TREC [7].

A standard IR test collection includes three elements: (1) document collection; (2) queries; and (3) relevance judgments for all the queries. Given such a test collection, a ranked list of search results for a query is often evaluated using several measures. The two basic measures are *precision* and *recall*. Precision is the percentage of relevant documents in the search results, while recall is the percentage of retrieved relevant documents in all the relevant documents in the entire collection.

Formally, let $X = \{D^1, ..., D^k\}$ be the set of search results where D^i is the i-th ranked document, and $Y = \{Y_1, ..., Y_{k'}\}$ be the set of all relevant documents for the query in the collection. We have:

$$precision = \frac{|X \cap Y|}{|X|} \quad recall = \frac{|X \cap Y|}{|Y|} \ .$$

Both precision and recall are defined with respect to a set of retrieved documents. Thus, given a ranked list of search results, we will need to choose a cutoff point to compute precision and recall. For example, precision at top ten documents is a measure frequently used to measure the accuracy in the top-ranked results, and is quite meaningful to a user because it indicates how many relevant documents a user can expect to see on the first page of search results (a web search engine usually shows ten results on each page of results).

However, precision at top k documents is insensitive to the change of the ranks of relevant documents among the top k documents, thus it is not a good measure for measuring the *overall* ranking accuracy. For comparing two ranked lists more accurately, IR researchers proposed another measure, called *average precision*, which is sensitive to any small change in the ranking of relevant documents. It is defined as follows:

$$avgprec = \frac{1}{k'} \sum_{i=1}^{k'} i/r_i \ ,$$

where r_i is the rank of the i-th *relevant* document in the search results. r_i is assumed to be infinite if the i-th relevant document is not retrieved. For example, if we have a total of 5 relevant documents, and the relevance status of the top 6 documents is $(+, +, -, -, -, +)$, where "+" (or "−") indicates the document at that rank is relevant (or nonrelevant), the precision would be 3/6=0.5, the recall would be 3/5=0.6, and the average precision would be

$$avgprec = (1/1 + 2/2 + 3/6 + 0 + 0)/5 = 0.5 \ .$$

When there is only one single relevant document for a query, the average precision would be equal to the reciprocal of the rank of that relevant document. In suche a case, the measure is often called reciprocal rank.

Since we typically experiment with a set of queries, we would take the mean of the average precision on each query and compute a Mean Average Precision (MAP)[2]. MAP has so far been the standard measure for evaluating ranking accuracy of a retrieval model.

Note that although MAP reflects retrieval precision, it favors results with high recall. This is because we assume the precision corresponding to a missed relevant document to be zero, which penalizes a low recall system harshly. In general, when we summarize a ranked list of results with one single precision number, we inevitably would have to make some assumption about the desired tradeoff between precision and recall because if we draw precision-recall curves over a wide range of cutoff points in the ranked list, one ranked list may have a higher precision at a low level of recall while another may have a better precision at a high level of recall.

One deficiency of MAP is that binary relevance is assumed. Intuitively, relevance can be judged at multiple levels (e.g., highly relevant, relevant, and nonrelevant). To measure the overall ranking accuracy of a retrieval system in case of multiple relevance levels, another measure called Normalized Discounted Cumulative Gain (NDCG) is often used [8]. It can be regarded as a generalization of precision at top k documents to accommodate multiple levels of relevance. It also gives a highly ranked document more weight, so it is sensitive to the internal ranking of the k documents.

The basic idea of NDCG is as follows. We assume that each document has an associated "gain" which corresponds to its relevance level; a highly relevant document would have a higher gain than a marginally relevant one. We then measure the overall ranking accuracy of the top k documents with the sum of the gains of the k documents (called cumulative gain). The measure NDCG further improves this basic idea in two ways: (1) It heuristically gives a higher weight to a highly ranked document to allow it to emphasize the importance of ranking the documents with high gain values on the very top of the ranked list[3]. The actual formula would achieve this by *discounting* the gain of a lowly ranked document. (2) It normalizes the overall discounted cumulative gain with its upper bound. The upper bound can be computed by assuming a perfect ranking of documents for the query. This makes the normalized discounted cumulative gain values more comparable across different queries; indeed, otherwise, the average value would be dominated by those from an easy query with many highly relevant documents.

After a system presents some search results to a user, sometimes the user is willing to provide some feedback on the relevance status of the results, i.e., telling the system which documents are relevant and which are not. In such a case, the retrieval system can learn from the examples of relevant and/or nonrelevant documents provided by the user to improve the search results. This is called *relevance feedback*, and is an important technique for improving search accuracy.

When the user is not willing to make judgments, which is often the case, the system may still perform feedback by simply assuming some top-ranked documents to be relevant and most other documents in the collection to be nonrelevant. This is called *pseudo relevance feedback* or simply

---

[2]The mean can be either an arithmetic mean or geometric mean. The former can be dominated by the performance of an easy query, while the latter better reflects the overall performance on difficult queries. When geometric mean is used, the measure is often abbreviated as GMAP.

[3]Note that MAP also naturally puts more weight on a top-ranked document.

pseudo feedback, and it also tends to improve retrieval performance on average, especially recall. But since the relevance information used is unreliable, pseudo feedback may hurt the performance for some queries, making it a major challenge in IR research to improve the robustness of pseudo feedback.

A third kind of feedback is to use user interactions (e.g., past queries, clickthroughs) to infer a user's interest and improve search results. This is called *implicit feedback* [9], and is generally effective. Implicit feedback is particularly powerful when a search system can collect a lot of user information from a large number of users, as is the case for Web search. Indeed, modern web search engines all take advantage of the massive amount of implicit feedback information to improve search results. More discussion about feedback can be found in [10]. In general, we would expect a retrieval model to be able to support all these different kinds of feedback.

1.2   STATISTICAL LANGUAGE MODELS

A statistical language model (or just language model for short) is a probability distribution over word sequences. It thus gives any sequence of words a potentially different probability. For example, a language model may give the following three word sequences different probabilities:

p("Today is Wednesday") $= 0.001$
p("Today Wednesday is") $= 0.000000001$
p("The equation has a solution") $= 0.000001$.

Clearly, a language model can be context dependent. In the language model shown above, the sequence "The equation has a solution" has a smaller probability than "Today is Wednesday." This may be a reasonable language model for describing general conversations, but it may be inaccurate for describing conversations happening at a mathematics conference, in which the sequence "The equation has a solution" may occur more frequently than "Today is Wednesday."

Given a language model, we can sample word sequences according to the distribution to obtain a text sample. In this sense, we may use such a model to "generate" text. Thus, a language model is also often called a generative model for text.

Why is a language model useful? A general answer is that it provides a principled way to quantify the uncertainties associated with the use of natural language. More specifically, it allows us to answer many interesting questions related to information retrieval. For example, a language model may help answering the question: how likely would a user use a query containing the word "baseball" if the user wants to find information about sports?

If we enumerate all the possible sequences of words and give a probability to each sequence, the model would be too complex to estimate because the number of parameters is potentially infinite since we have potentially infinite number of word sequences. That is, we would never have enough data to estimate these parameters. Thus, we always have to make assumptions to simplify the model. The simplest language model is the *unigram language model* in which we assume that a word sequence is generated by generating each word *independently*. Thus, the probability of a sequence of words would be equal to the product of the probability of each word.

Formally, let V be the set of words in the vocabulary, and $w_1...w_n$ a word sequence, where $w_i \in V$ is a word. We have:

$$p(w_1...w_n) = \prod_{i=1}^{n} p(w_i) .$$

It is easy to see that given a unigram language model θ, we have as many parameters as the words in the vocabulary, i.e., $\{p(w_i|\theta)\}_{i=1}^{|V|}$, and they satisfy the constraint $\sum_{i=1}^{|V|} p(w_i|\theta) = 1$. Such a model essentially specifies a multinomial distribution over all the words.

Clearly, given a language model θ, in general, the probabilities of generating two different documents D_1 and D_2, would be different, i.e., $p(D_1|\theta) \neq p(D_2|\theta)$. What kind of documents would have higher probabilities? Intuitively it would be those documents that contain many occurrences of the high probability words according to θ. In this sense, the high probability words of θ can indicate the topic captured by θ.

For example, the two unigram language models illustrated in Figure 1.1 suggest a topic about "text mining" and a topic about "health", respectively. Intuitively, if D is a text mining paper, we would expect $p(D|\theta_1) > p(D|\theta_2)$, while if D' is a blog article discussing diet control, we would expect $p(D'|\theta_2) > p(D'|\theta_1)$. We can also expect $p(D|\theta_1) > p(D'|\theta_1)$ and $p(D|\theta_2) < p(D'|\theta_2)$.

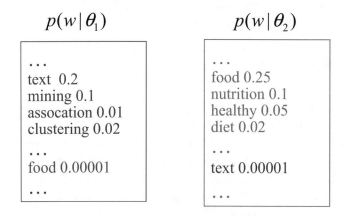

Figure 1.1: Illustration of two unigram language models capturing the topics "text mining" (θ_1) and "health" (θ_2), respectively.

Now suppose we have observed a document D (e.g., a short abstract of a text mining paper) which is assumed to be generated using a unigram language model θ, and we would like to infer the θ (i.e., estimate the probability of each word w, $p(w|\theta)$) based on the observed D. This is a standard problem in statistics (i.e., parameter estimation) and can be solved using many different methods.

One popular method is the maximum likelihood (ML) estimator, which seeks a model $\hat{\theta}$ that would give the observed data the highest likelihood (i.e., best explain the data):

$$\hat{\theta} = \arg\max_{\theta} p(D|\theta) .$$

It is easy to show that the ML estimate of a unigram language model gives each word a probability equal to its relative frequency in D. That is,

$$p(w|\hat{\theta}) \;=\; \frac{c(w, D)}{|D|} , \tag{1.1}$$

where $c(w, D)$ is the count of word w in D and $|D|$ is the length of D, or total number of words in D.

To see why, we can write down the log-likelihood function as follows:

$$\log p(D|\theta) = \sum_{w \in V} c(w, D) \log p(w|\theta) .$$

To compute the ML estimate is to find values of $p(w|\theta)$ to maximize this likelihood function subject to the constraint $\sum_{w \in V} p(w|\theta) = 1$.

Using the Lagrange Multiplier approach [11], we would introduce a new variable λ (called Lagrange multiplier) to combine the constraint with the original log-likelihood function so as to convert the original *constrained* optimization problem into a new *unconstrained* optimization problem in which we want to find an optimal θ and an optimal λ to maximize the following function:

$$\sum_{w \in V} c(w, D) \log p(w|\theta) + \lambda \left(1 - \sum_{w \in V} p(w|\theta) \right) .$$

Taking partial derivatives of this function with respect to $p(w|\theta)$ and λ and setting the derivatives to zero, we can then obtain the solution for θ as shown in Equation 1.1.

Because the ML estimate attempts to fit the data as much as possible, it may "over-fit" the data if the data is a small sample. Indeed, it would give any word not seen in D a zero probability, which may not be reasonable especially if D is a small sample. Why do we believe assigning zero probability to all the unseen words is unreasonable? This has to do with our prior belief of what a word distribution characterizing the topic of a document should look like; intuitively, had the author decided to write a longer document D, we would probably have been able to observe some of those unseen words. The *Bayesian estimator* would seek a model that can both maximize the data likelihood and reflect our prior belief about the model.

For example, the Maximum A Posteriori (MAP) estimator would maximize the posterior probability $p(\theta|D)$, i.e.,

$$\hat{\theta} = \arg\max_{\theta} p(\theta|D) = \arg\max_{\theta} p(D|\theta) p(\theta) .$$

Naturally, we need to define our prior $p(\theta)$; with different priors, we generally would obtain different estimates. If our prior $p(\theta)$ strongly prefers a model that does not give zero probability to any word, the ultimate estimated model $\hat{\theta}$ would "listen" to the prior and not assign zero probability to any word. Adjusting the ML estimate to avoid zero probability is often called "smoothing." There are many different methods for smoothing a unigram language model which we will discuss later in the book.

Although unigram language models are simple, they clearly make unrealistic assumptions about word occurrences in text. For example, if an author has started using a word in writing an article, the author would tend to use the same word again, which means that the probability of seeing the first occurrence of a word is intuitively different (smaller) than the probability of seeing a repeated occurrence of the same word. Also, if we have seen the word "software" in a document, the probability of seeing a related word such as "program" would be much higher than if we have not seen "software" in the document.

More sophisticated language models have thus been developed to address the limitations of unigram language models. For example, an n-gram language model would capture some limited dependency between words and assume the occurrence of a word depends on the proceeding $n - 1$ words. As a specific example, a bigram language model is defined as follows:

$$p(w_1...w_n) = p(w_1) \prod_{i=2}^{n} p(w_i | w_{i-1}) \, .$$

Such a bigram language model can capture any potential local dependency between two adjacent words.

There are also language models capturing remote dependencies through "triggers" [12]. Perhaps the most sophisticated language model is defined through a probabilistic context-free grammar; such a language model is explicitly structured based on the grammar of a language [13]. More in-depth discussion about such language models can be found in [12, 14].

While theoretically speaking, we would like to adopt a sophisticated language model that can model our language more accurately, in reality, we often have to make a tradeoff. This is because as the complexity of a language model increases, so does the number of parameters. As a result, we would need much more data to estimate the parameters. With limited amount of data, our estimate of parameters would not be accurate. The computational cost of complex language models is also a concern for all large-scale retrieval applications.

So far, the simplest unigram language model has been shown to be quite effective for information retrieval, while more sophisticated language models such as bigram language models or trigram language models tend not to improve much over the unigram language model. One reason may be because of the problem of data sparseness, which makes the estimated complex language models inaccurate. From retrieval perspective, the nonpromising performance of complex language models may also be related to nonoptimal weighting of bigrams and trigrams; indeed, when they are combined with unigrams, we must avoid over-rewarding matching multiple words in a phrase [15].

Another reason why unigram language models seem to perform very well is because the retrieval task is a relatively "easy" task compared with some other language understanding tasks such as machine translation in the sense that information about word presence or absence and word frequencies may be sufficient to determine the relevance of a document while the exact word order may not be so important (as, e.g., in the case of machine translation). For machine translation, unigram language models are clearly insufficient and more sophisticated language models would be needed [16]. Also, for speech recognition, modeling word order is obviously very important [14].

How to evaluate a language model depends on the purpose of modeling. In information retrieval, what we care about is how effective a language model is for retrieval. Thus, we would use a language model for ranking documents and evaluate the accuracy of ranking. That is, we would evaluate a language model based on its contribution to retrieval accuracy. This is an *indirect* way of evaluating the quality of a language model because we assess a language model together with other components of a retrieval system, and the retrieval performance we see can be potentially affected by many other factors, not just the language model.

Since a language model is a probabilistic model of text data, a more *direct* way of evaluating a language model would be to assess how well the model fits the data to be modeled (i.e., test data). For example, we may compute the likelihood of the test data given a model to be evaluated; a higher likelihood would indicate a better fit, thus a better language model.

Note that the relative performance of two language models may be different when using these two different evaluation strategies. This is because there may be some "gap" between the task and the language model; as a result, fitting the data well does not always imply better performance for the task. A main goal in research on using language models for retrieval is to design appropriate retrieval models so that an improved language model (improved in terms of direct evaluation) would also lead to improved performance for the retrieval task. If such correlation exists, we would have some guidance on how to find a better retrieval model –we may find a better retrieval model through improving language models and/or estimation of language models. As we will discuss in detail later, we can indeed improve retrieval accuracy through various ways to improve the estimate of language models used for ranking documents.

CHAPTER 2

Overview of Information Retrieval Models

Over the decades, many different retrieval models have been proposed, studied, and tested. Their mathematical basis spans a large spectrum, including algebra, logic, probability, and statistics. In this chapter, we briefly review all the major retrieval models to give readers a picture about how language models are connected with other retrieval models.

We will group these models into five categories based on how they define/measure relevance. In the first category, relevance is assumed to be correlated with the similarity between a query and a document. In the second category, a binary random variable is used to model relevance and probabilistic models are used to estimate the value of this relevance variable. In the third category, relevance is modeled by the uncertainty of inferring queries from documents or vice versa. In the fourth category, relevance is captured through formally defined constraints on retrieval functions. In the fifth category, the retrieval problem is formalized generally as a statistical decision problem and relevance is regarded as part of a loss/utility function that affects retrieval decisions. We now discuss these categories in detail.

2.1 SIMILARITY-BASED MODELS

In a similarity-based retrieval model, it is assumed that the relevance status of a document with respect to a query is correlated with the *similarity* between the query and the document at some level of representation; the more similar to a query a document is, the more relevant the document is assumed to be. In practice, we can use any similarity measure that preserves such a correlation to generate a relevance status value (RSV) for each document and rank documents accordingly.

The vector space model is the most well-known model of this type [23, 24, 25]. In the vector space model, a document and a query are represented as two term vectors in a high-dimensional term space. Each term is assigned a weight that reflects its "importance" to the document or the query. Given a query, the relevance status value of a document is given by the similarity between the query vector and document vector as measured by some vector similarity measure, such as the dot product of the two vectors or the cosine of the angle formed by the two vectors.

Formally, a document D may be represented by a document vector $\vec{D} = (x_1, x_2, ..., x_M)$, where M is the total number of terms in our vocabulary, and x_i is the weight assigned to word w_i. Similarly, a query Q can be represented by a query vector $\vec{Q} = (y_1, y_2, ..., y_M)$. The weight is usually computed based on the so-called TF-IDF weighting, which is a combination of three factors [26]:

(1) the local frequency of the term (in a document or query); (2) the global frequency of the term in the whole collection; and (3) document length.

The vector space model is by far the most popular retrieval model due to its simplicity and effectiveness. The following is a typical effective weighting formula with pivoted document length normalization taken from [26]:

$$\sum_{t \in Q, D} \frac{1 + \ln(1 + \ln(tf))}{(1 - s) + s \frac{dl}{avdl}} \times qtf \times \ln \frac{N + 1}{df}$$

where s is an empirical parameter (usually 0.20), and

tf is the term's frequency in document
qtf is the term's frequency in query
N is the total number of documents in the collection
df is the number of documents that contain the term
dl is the document length, and
$avdl$ is the average document length.

In the formula above, the term $\ln \frac{N+1}{df}$ is called the Inverse Document Frequency (IDF), which penalizes a term that is common in the collection (intuitively, matching a rare term is "worth" more than matching a common one). IDF, proposed by Sparck Jones [27], is a very important retrieval heuristic which tends to show up in all effective retrieval functions in one way or another. The term with tf, document length, and parameter s is a normalized form of Term Frequency (TF) which rewards matching a term more times in a document. More discussion about retrieval heuristics can be found in [28].

The vector space model naturally decomposes a retrieval model into three components: (1) a term vector representation of query; (2) a term vector representation of document; and (3) a similarity/distance measure of the document vector and the query vector. However, the "synchronization" among the three components is generally unspecified; in particular, the similarity measure does not dictate the representation of a document or query. Thus, the vector space model is actually a general retrieval *framework*, in which the representation of query and documents as well as the similarity measure can all be arbitrary in principle.

Related to its generality, the vector space model can also be regarded as a procedural model of retrieval, in which the task of retrieval is naturally divided into two separate stages: indexing and search. The indexing stage explicitly has to do with representing the document and the query by the "indexing terms" extracted from the document and the query. The indexing terms are often assigned different weights to indicate their importance in describing a document or a query. The search stage has to do with evaluating the relevance value (i.e., the similarity) between a document vector and a query vector. The flexibility of the vector space model makes it easy to incorporate different indexing models. For example, the 2-Poisson probabilistic indexing model can be used to select indexing terms and/or assign term weights [29, 30]. Latent semantic indexing [31] and Probabilistic Latent Semantic Indexing [32] can be applied to reduce the dimension of the term space and to capture the semantic "closeness" among terms, and thus to improve the representation of the documents and query. A document can also be represented by a multinomial distribution over the terms, as in the distribution model of indexing proposed in [33], which would later be heavily used in the language modeling approaches.

In the vector space model, feedback (see Section 1.1) is typically treated as query vector updating. A well-known approach is the Rocchio method, which simply adds the centroid vector of the relevant documents to the query vector and subtracts from it the centroid vector of the nonrelevant documents with appropriate coefficients [34]. Thus, assuming that D_R and D_N are the sets of relevant and nonrelevant documents, the updated query vector would be:

$$\vec{Q}' = \alpha \vec{Q} + \beta \frac{1}{|D_R|} \sum_{d \in D_R} \vec{d} - \gamma \frac{1}{|D_N|} \sum_{d \in D_N} \vec{d} .$$

In effect, this leads to an expansion of the original query vector, i.e., additional terms are extracted from the known relevant (and nonrelevant) documents, and are added to the original query vector with appropriate weights [35].

The extended Boolean (p-norm) model is a heuristic extension of the traditional Boolean model to perform document ranking, but it can also be regarded as a special case of the similarity model [36, 37]. In the traditional Boolean retrieval model, a query specifies a Boolean condition that a relevant document must satisfy (e.g., (HasTerm "computer") AND (HasTerm "virus")). Documents satisfying the query condition would be retrieved as search results. One deficiency of the Boolean retrieval model is that it does not provide a score for ranking, but ranking may be desirable. For example, if a query has three conjunctive term constraints, intuitively, a document that satisfies two of them is better than one that satisfies only one of them. To address this issue, the extended Boolean model defines a similarity function with a parameter p to control the "strictness" of satisfying the constraint of a Boolean query. The function behaves in such a way that it would approach a strict (conjunctive or disjunctive) Boolean model when p approaches infinity, but would soften the conjunctive or disjunctive constraint and behave more like a regular vector space similarity measure as p becomes smaller. Thus, the extended Boolean model provides a very interesting, flexible way to rank documents for a Boolean query. However, the model must rely on some assumptions about the Boolean structure of a query, which is not always available, and it has some undesirable mathematical properties (e.g., the score may not change monotonically as p changes) [38]. There has also been little, if any, large-scale evaluation of the model.

The main criticism for the vector space model is that it provides no guidance for the choice of representation, making the study of representation inherently separate from the relevance estimation. The separation of the relevance function from the weighting of terms has the advantage of being flexible, but makes it very difficult to study the interaction of representation and relevance measurement. The semantics of a similarity/relevance function is highly dependent on the actual representation (i.e., term weights) of the query and the document. As a result, the study of representation in the vector space model has been so far largely heuristic.

The two central problems in document and query representation are the extraction of indexing terms/units and the weighting of the indexing terms. The choice of different indexing units has been extensively studied, but for English, early experiments did not show significant improvement over the simplest word-based indexing [39]. Some more recent evaluation has shown more promising improvement on average through using linguistic phrases, but the improvement is inconsistent—some queries are improved, but others are not [40, 41, 42]. For many non-English languages, morphological normalization and phrases have been shown to be clearly beneficial [43, 44].

Many heuristics have been proposed to improve term weighting, but no weighting method has been found to be significantly better than the heuristic TF-IDF term weighting [45]. To address the variances in the length of documents, an effective weighting formula also needs to incorporate document length heuristically [46].

Salton et al. introduced the idea of the discrimination value of an indexing term [47]. The discrimination value of an indexing term is the increase or the decrease in the mean inter-document distance caused by adding the indexing term to the term space for text representation. They found that the middle frequency terms have a higher discrimination value. Given a similarity measure, the discrimination value provides a principled way of selecting terms for indexing. However, there are still two deficiencies. First, the discrimination value is not modeling relevance, but rather, relies on a given similarity measure. Second, it is only helpful for selecting indexing terms, but not for the weighting of terms.

The divergence from randomness model proposed in [48] offers some new insights into term weighting in the vector space model and provides a probabilistic justification for a number of weighting methods. Some of them are shown to be very effective in TREC evaluation [48].

The development of language modeling approaches has led to a new family of similarity-based models in which scoring is based on the Kullback-Leibler (KL) divergence (or equivalently cross entropy) of a query language model and a document language model [1]. Because the document and query representations are based on language models, term weighting can be addressed through statistical estimation. The KL-divergence model thus provides more guidance on how to improve a retrieval function than the traditional vector-space model.

2.2   PROBABILISTIC RELEVANCE MODELS

In a probabilistic relevance model, we are interested in the question "What is the probability that *this* document is relevant to *this* query?" [49]. Given a query, a document is assumed to be either relevant or nonrelevant, but a system can never be sure about the true relevance status of a document, so it has to rely on a probabilistic relevance model to estimate it.

Such a retrieval strategy can be justified by the Probability Ranking Principle (PRP) [50], which is often taken as the foundation for probabilistic retrieval models. As stated in [50], the principle is based on the following two assumptions:

"(a) The *relevance* of a document to a request is independent of the other documents in the collection;

(b) The *usefulness* of a relevant document to a requester may depend on the *number* of relevant documents the requester has already seen (the more he has seen, the less useful a subsequent one may be)."

Under these assumptions, the PRP provides a justification for ranking documents in descending order of probability of relevance, which can be evaluated separately for each document.

Formally, let random variables D and Q denote a document and query, respectively. Let R be a binary random variable that indicates whether D is relevant to Q or not. It takes two values which we denote as r ("relevant") and $\bar{r}$ ("not relevant"). The task is to estimate the probability of relevance, i.e., $p(R = r \mid D, Q)$. Depending on how this probability is estimated, there are several special cases of this general probabilistic relevance model.

First, $p(R = r \mid D, Q)$ can be estimated *directly* using a discriminative (regression) model. Essentially, the relevance variable R is assumed to be dependent on "features" that characterize the matching of D and Q (e.g., the number of matched terms). In general, suppose we have k features, $F_i(Q, D), i = 1, ..., k$, defined on the query-document pair (Q, D). We will assume that there exists a function f with parameters Λ such that

$$p(R = r \mid D, Q) = f(F_1(Q, D), ..., F_k(Q, D), \Lambda) .$$

With training examples of the form (Q, D, r) (D is relevant to Q) and $(Q, D, \bar{r})$ (D is not relevant to Q), we can then fit such a function to the training examples to maximize the likelihood of the training data or minimize the errors on ranking the training examples.

Early work in this direction includes linear regression [36], polynomial regression [51], and logistic regression [52]. Such regression models provide a principled way of exploring heuristic features and ideas. One important advantage of regression models is their ability to learn from all the past relevance judgments including judgments for different queries. However, because regression models are based on heuristic features in the first place, lots of empirical experimentation would be needed in order to find a set of good features. In this sense, a regression model provides only limited guidance for extending a retrieval model.

Before Web search was popular, the retrieval problems studied often involved simple free-text documents. With TF-IDF weighting being the main basis for designing effective features, these regression models have not been able to show real advantages over a well-tuned vector space model. Recently, however, such models have regained much attention due to the need for combining *many* different features (e.g., content scores, link-based scores, anchor text scores) for effective Web search [53]; recent work in this direction has strong machine learning flavor and the models are often phrased as "learning to rank" in contrast to many other applications of machine learning where the goal is "learning to classify" (objects). These new models are more successful than the old regression models explored earlier [36, 51, 52] because they leverage the scores given by other state of the art retrieval models as features and combine them with additional useful features such as link information for web pages.

For example, the Markov Random Field (MRF) model proposed in [54] can easily combine features corresponding matching documents with queries at different granularities of units, including both single terms and term-dependency structures (e.g., co-occurring terms within a window of text, which can capture proximity of terms), and this model has been shown to perform very well [54]. However, a common weakness of all these discriminative models remains the lack of guidance on designing effective features.

Alternatively, $p(R = r \mid D, Q)$ can be estimated *indirectly* using a generative model in the following way [55]:

$$p(R = r \mid D, Q) \;=\; \frac{p(D, Q \mid R = r)\, p(R = r)}{p(D, Q)}.$$

Equivalently, we may use the following log-odds ratio to rank documents:

$$\log \frac{p(r \mid D, Q)}{p(\bar{r} \mid D, Q)} \;=\; \log \frac{p(D, Q \mid r)\, p(r)}{p(D, Q \mid \bar{r})\, p(\bar{r})}.$$

There are two different ways to factor the conditional probability $p(D, Q \mid R)$, corresponding to "document generation" and "query generation."

With document generation, $p(D, Q \mid R) = p(D \mid Q, R)p(Q \mid R)$, so we end up with the following ranking formula:

$$\log \frac{p(r \mid D, Q)}{p(\bar{r} \mid D, Q)} = \log \frac{p(D \mid Q, r)}{p(D \mid Q, \bar{r})} + \log \frac{p(r \mid Q)}{p(\bar{r} \mid Q)}.$$

Essentially, the retrieval problem is formulated as a two-category document classification problem, although we are only interested in ranking the classification likelihood, rather than actually assigning class labels. Operationally, two models are estimated for each query, one modeling relevant documents, the other modeling nonrelevant documents. Documents are then ranked according to the posterior probability of relevance.

Most classical probabilistic retrieval models [56, 57, 58] are based on document generation. The Binary Independence Retrieval (BIR) model [56, 58] is perhaps the most well-known classical probabilistic model. The model assumes that terms are independently distributed in each of the two relevance models, so it essentially uses the Naïve Bayes classifier for document ranking [59][1]. The BIR retrieval formula is the following [56, 55]:

$$\log \frac{p(r \mid D, Q)}{p(\bar{r} \mid D, Q)} \overset{\text{rank}}{=} \sum_{T \in D \cap T \in Q} \log \frac{p(T = 1 \mid Q, r)(1 - p(T = 1 \mid Q, \bar{r}))}{(1 - p(T = 1 \mid Q, r))p(T = 1 \mid Q, \bar{r})},$$

where $\overset{\text{rank}}{=}$ means equivalent in terms of being used for ranking documents, and $p(T = 1 \mid Q, r)$ and $p(T = 1 \mid Q, \bar{r})$ are probabilities of seeing term T in a relevant document and nonrelevant document,

---

[1]The required underlying independence assumption for the final retrieval formula is actually weaker [60].

respectively. Note that in this model, we only model presence and absence of words in a relevant or nonrelevant document and thus ignore the frequency counts of words. In other words, we assume a multiple Bernoulli event model and observe constraints: $p(T = 1 \mid Q, r) + p(T = 0 \mid Q, r) = 1$ and $p(T = 1 \mid Q, \bar{r}) + p(T = 0 \mid Q, \bar{r}) = 1$.

There have been several efforts to improve the binary representation. Van Rijsbergen extended the binary independence model by capturing some term-dependency as defined by a minimum-spanning tree weighted by average mutual information [61]. The dependency model achieved significant increases in retrieval performance over the independence model. However, the evaluation was only done on very small collections, and the estimation of many more parameters is a problem in practice [62]. Croft investigated how the heuristic term significance weight can be incorporated into probabilistic models in a principled way [63]. Another effort to improve document representation involves introducing the term frequency directly into the model by using a multiple 2-Poisson mixture representation of documents [64]. A different way of introducing the term frequency into the model, not directly proposed but implied by a lot of work in text categorization, is to regard a document as being generated from a multinomial unigram language model [65, 66]. The relationship between different event models of the document-generation model is discusses in [206].

In general, with examples of relevant and nonrelevant documents, we can easily estimate the parameters in a document-generation model. Specifically, in the document-generation model, we need to estimate two component models $p(D|Q, r)$ and $p(D|Q, \bar{r})$. The first can be estimated based on examples of relevant documents, while the second can be estimated based on examples of nonrelevant documents. Thus, the document-generation model is quite natural for relevance feedback. However, it was found that for feedback, it may be better to selectively use only some of the most useful terms instead of using all the terms, and the Offer Weight heuristic measure was recommended to be used for selecting such terms [67].

Without relevant examples, however, estimation of parameters can be difficult [68, 69]; thus, heuristics may be needed to make such a model useful for ad hoc retrieval without relevance feedback information. For example, an approximation of the 2-Poisson mixture model using a simple TF formula has led to a quite effective retrieval function (i.e., BM25 [70]). This function was first successfully used in City University's Okapi system and later recognized as one of the most effective and robust retrieval functions. The BM25 formula is shown below, following the notations used in [26]:

$$\sum_{t \in Q, D} \ln \frac{N - df + 0.5}{df + 0.5} \times \frac{(k_1 + 1)tf}{k_1((1 - b) + b\frac{dl}{avdl}) + tf} \times \frac{(k_3 + 1)qtf}{k_3 + qtf}$$

where, $k_1 \in [1.0, 2.0]$, b (usually 0.75), and $k_3 \in [0, 1000]$ are parameters, and other variables have the same meaning as in the vector space retrieval formula described in the previous section[2].

To solve the parameter estimation problem in the document-generation model, Lavrenko and Croft have developed a relevance model which essentially implements the idea of pseudo feedback,

---

[2]The original formula presented in [26] has a typo in the denominator of the TF normalization part, which has been corrected here.

and it enables model estimation without relevance judgments [71]. This model has been shown to be quite effective, and will be discussed in detail in Section 5.3.3.

So far, we have considered the case of refining the probabilistic model with document generation. Let us now consider refining it with query generation: $p(D, Q \mid R) = p(Q \mid D, R)p(D \mid R)$. In this case, we end up with the following ranking formula:

$$\log \frac{p(r \mid D, Q)}{p(\bar{r} \mid D, Q)} \stackrel{\text{rank}}{=} \log \frac{p(Q \mid D, r)}{p(Q \mid D, \bar{r})} + \log \frac{p(r \mid D)}{p(\bar{r} \mid D)} \; .$$

Under the assumption that conditioned on the event $R = \bar{r}$, the document D is independent of the query Q, i.e., $p(D, Q \mid R = \bar{r}) = p(D \mid R = \bar{r})p(Q \mid R = \bar{r})$, the formula becomes

$$\log \frac{p(r \mid D, Q)}{p(\bar{r} \mid D, Q)} \stackrel{\text{rank}}{=} \log p(Q \mid D, r) + \log \frac{p(r \mid D)}{p(\bar{r} \mid D)} \; .$$

There are two components in this model. The major component $p(Q \mid D, r)$ can be interpreted as a "relevant query model" conditioned on a document. That is, $p(Q \mid D, r)$ is the probability that a user, who likes document D, would use Q as a query to retrieve D. The second component $p(r \mid D)$ is a prior that can be used to encode any bias on documents.

Models based on query generation have been explored in [72], [58], and [73]. The probabilistic indexing model proposed in [72] is the first probabilistic retrieval model, in which the indexing terms assigned to a document are weighted by the probability that a user who likes the document would use the term in the query. That is, the weight of term t for document D is $p(t \mid D, r)$. However, the estimation of the model is based on the user's feedback, not the content of D. The Binary Independence Indexing (BII) model proposed in [58] is another special case of the query generation model. It allows the description of a document (with weighted terms) to be estimated based on arbitrary queries, but the specific parameterization makes it hard to estimate all the parameters in practice.

The query generation derivation above suggests that we can score documents based on query likelihood $p(Q \mid D, r)$ if we use a noninformative (i.e., uniform) prior $p(r \mid D)$. This is precisely the so-called language modeling approach to retrieval, which was first introduced in [74] and independently explored in some TREC work [75, 76]. This language modeling approach (i.e., the query likelihood scoring method) has since attracted much attention, and many interesting and effective variant models have been proposed. Compared with the traditional retrieval models, including both the vector-space model and the classical probabilistic model, the language modeling approaches put more emphasis on parameter estimation and thus provide more guidance on term weighting. They are empirically as effective as any other existing model and can often be easily extended/adapted to model complex retrieval tasks. The main purpose of this book is to introduce and review this new generation of probabilistic retrieval models and their extensions.

Instead of imposing a strict document generation or query generation decomposition of $p(D, Q \mid R)$, one can also "generate" a document-query pair simultaneously. Mittendorf & Schauble explored a passage-based generative model using the Hidden Markov Model (HMM), which can be regarded as such a case [77]. In this work, a document query pair is represented as a sequence of symbols, each corresponding to a term in a particular position of the document. All term tokens are clustered based on the similarity between the token and the query. In this way, a term token in a particular position of a document can be mapped to a symbol that represents the cluster the token belongs to. Such symbol sequences are modeled as the output from an HMM with two states, one corresponding to relevant passage and the other the background noise. The relevance value is then computed based on the likelihood ratio of the sequence given the passage HMM model and the background model.

2.3   PROBABILISTIC INFERENCE MODELS

In a probabilistic inference model, the uncertainty whether a document is relevance to a query is modeled by the uncertainty associated with inferring/proving the query from the document. Depending on how one defines what it means to "prove a query from a document," different inference models are possible.

Van Rijsbergen introduced a logic-based probabilistic inference model for text retrieval [78], in which, a document is relevant to a query if and only if the query can be proved from the document. The Boolean retrieval model can be regarded as a simple case of this model. Specifically, we may regard both a query and a document as consisting of a set of propositions such as "HasTerm(computer)" and "HasTerm(virus)." Thus, a query "computer virus" can be represented as the following conjunctive expression:

$$HasTerm(computer) \text{ AND } HasTerm(virus).$$

Similarly, we can represent a document in this way. If we can prove that the query expression logically follows a document expression, it would mean that the document indeed contains both query terms, thus it is relevant.

A main limitation of the Boolean retrieval model is that it does not consider uncertainty in relevance. To cope with the inherent uncertainty in relevance, Van Rijsbergen introduced a logic for probabilistic inference, in which the probability of a conditional, such as $p \rightarrow q$, can be estimated based on the notion of possible worlds. In [79], Wong and Yao extended the probabilistic inference model and developed a general probabilistic inference model which subsumes several other retrieval models such as Boolean, vector space, and the classic probabilistic models. In [80], Fuhr shows that some particular form of the language modeling approach can also be derived as a special case of the general probabilistic inference model.

While theoretically interesting, the probabilistic inference models all must rely on further assumptions about the representation of documents and queries in order to obtain an *operational* retrieval formula. The choice of such representations is in a way outside the model, so there is little guidance on how to choose or how to improve a representation.

The inference network model is also based on probabilistic inference [81]. It is essentially a Bayesian belief network that models the dependency between the satisfaction of a query and the observation of documents. The estimation of relevance is based on the computation of the conditional probability that the query is satisfied given that the document is observed. Other similar uses of the Bayesian belief network in retrieval are presented in [82, 83, 84]. The inference network model is a much more general formalism than most of the models that we have discussed above. With different ways to realize the probabilistic relationship between the observation of documents and the satisfaction of the user's information need, one can obtain many different existing specific retrieval models, such as Boolean, extended Boolean, vector space, and conventional probabilistic models. More importantly, the inference network model can potentially go beyond the traditional notion of topical relevance; indeed, the goal of inference is a very general one, and at its highest level, the framework is so general that it can accommodate almost any probabilistic model. The generality makes it possible to combine multiple evidence, including different formulations of the same query. The query language based directly on the model has been an important and practical contribution to IR technology.

However, despite its generality, the inference network framework says little about how one can further decompose the general probabilistic model. As a result, operationally, one usually has to set probabilities based on heuristics, as was done in the Inquery system [85].

Kwok's network model may also be considered as performing a probabilistic inference [86], although it is based on spreading activation.

In general, the probabilistic inference models address the issue of relevance in a very general way. In some sense, the lack of a commitment to specific assumptions in these general models has helped to maintain their generality as retrieval models. But this also deprives them of "predictive power" as a theory. As a result, they generally provide little guidance on how to refine the general notion of relevance.

2.4   AXIOMATIC RETRIEVAL FRAMEWORK

The three categories of retrieval models discussed above all have some retrieval parameters that have to be tuned in order to obtain optimal retrieval performance. Although when well tuned, these models can all be empirically effective, their performance can be poor if the retrieval parameter is not set optimally. It also seems that virtually all these models eventually lead to some retrieval function that implements TF-IDF weighting and document length normalization. Moreover, these weighting heuristics also must be implemented in some special functional forms in order for a retrieval function to perform well. These observations suggest that there may be some "essential properties" that an effective retrieval function must satisfy, and if these properties are satisfied, the exact form of the retrieval function really does not matter.

In [28], the three major retrieval heuristics (i.e., TF, IDF, and length normalization) are formally characterized with well-defined constraints on retrieval functions. For example, the following Term Frequency Constraints capture the TF heuristic:

TFC1: Let $q = w$ be a query with only one term w. Let d_1 and d_2 be two documents with identical length, i.e., $|d_1| = |d_2|$. If word w occurs more times in d_1 than in d_2, i.e., $c(w, d_1) > c(w, d_2)$, then a retrieval function must give d_1 a higher score than d_2, i.e., $f(d_1, q) > f(d_2, q)$ for any retrieval function f.

TFC2: Let $q = w$ be a query with only one term w. Let d_1, d_2, and d_3 be three documents with identical length, i.e., $|d_1| = |d_2| = |d_3|$. Suppose $c(w, d_1) > 0$. If $c(w, d_2) - c(w, d_1) = 1$ and $c(w, d_3) - c(w, d_2) = 1$, then $f(d_2, q) - f(d_1, q) > f(d_3, q) - f(d_2, q)$ for any retrieval function f.

Intuitively, the first constraint simply says that a document matching a query term more times should be scored higher (i.e., the first partial derivative of the retrieval function with respect to the TF variable should be positive). The second constraint ensures that the increase in score due to an increase in TF is smaller for larger TFs (i.e., the second partial derivative with respect to the TF variable should be negative). Here, the intuition is that the change in score caused by increasing TF from 1 to 2 should be larger than that caused by increasing TF from 100 to 101.

As another example, we can also define the following constraint to regulate the behavior of a retrieval function with respect to the length of documents.

LNC2: Let q be a query. $\forall k > 1$, if d_1 and d_2 are two documents such that $|d_1| = k \cdot |d_2|$ and for all terms w, $c(w, d_1) = k \cdot c(w, d_2)$, then $f(d_1, q) \geq f(d_2, q)$ for any retrieval function.

This constraint says that if we concatenate a document with itself k times to form a new document, then the score of the new document should not be lower than the original document.

In [28], a total of 7 such constraints are defined, and it is shown that the empirical performance of a retrieval function is indeed correlated with whether it satisfies these constraints. For example, the pivoted length normalization retrieval function [46, 26] is shown to violate the LNC2 constraint defined above if the parameter s is too large ($s > 0.4$), and indeed, its empirical performance would drop significantly when $s > 0.4$. Language modeling retrieval functions are also shown to only conditionally satisfy this constraint when the parameter is in some range.

Since intuitively all reasonable retrieval functions must satisfy such constraints, we may regard these constraints as axioms for a retrieval function. Indeed, this suggests a general axiomatic framework to study and analyze retrieval functions. Specifically, we can define as many such constraints as possible and use them to guide us in finding an effective retrieval function. That is, we would look for a retrieval function that can satisfy all the desirable constraints. For example, we can take a generate-and-test strategy and systematically test a set of candidate retrieval functions. For each candidate retrieval function, we would check whether it satisfies the defined constraints; if it does not satisfy a constraint, we would then try to modify the function to make it satisfy the constraint. We can repeat this process until we find one that satisfies all the constraints.

In [87] and [88], such an axiomatic retrieval framework has been successfully leveraged to derive some interesting new retrieval functions that are more robust than existing retrieval functions as well as some retrieval functions that can incorporate semantic similarities of words to support semantic matching between queries and documents.

The axiomatic retrieval framework offers a novel way for exploring and comparing different retrieval models, but the framework does not provide constructive guidance on what candidate functions to explore. Thus, currently we still need to rely on existing retrieval models to suggest a tractable search space [87]. As will be discussed in the next section, language models naturally offer many alternative ways to model the retrieval problem. Thus, they can potentially supply candidate functions for axiomatic analysis.

2.5   DECISION-THEORETIC RETRIEVAL FRAMEWORK

All the retrieval models and retrieval functions we have discussed so far formulate the retrieval problem as to compute a score for *one* query and *one* document. Such a formulation is limited because we would not be able to model the redundancy among search results. A more general way of framing the retrieval problem is to take it as a decision problem in which a system would respond to a query by choosing a set of documents from a collection and presenting the documents in a certain way. Such a decision-theoretic view of retrieval has been formalized with Bayesian decision theory in [1, 89, 90], resulting in a general *risk minimization* framework for information retrieval. This framework also provides a general way to apply language models to information retrieval. Specifically, language models are naturally introduced to model the observed data, particularly documents and queries, in a statistical decision framework. We now present this framework in some detail.

To cast the retrieval problem as a decision optimization problem, we first need to model the observed data, which mainly consist of the documents and queries, but can also potentially include the user and the source of the documents. We naturally use language models to model documents and queries.

Formally, let θ_Q denote the parameters of a query model, and let θ_D denote the parameters of a document model. A user $\mathcal{U}$ generates a query by first selecting θ_Q, according to a distribution $p(\theta_Q \,|\, \mathcal{U})$. Using this model, a query Q is then generated with probability $p(Q \,|\, \theta_Q)$. Similarly, the source selects a document model θ_D according to a distribution $p(\theta_D \,|\, \mathcal{S})$, and then uses this model to generate a document D according to $p(D \,|\, \theta_D)$. See Figure 2.1 for an illustration of this generation process.

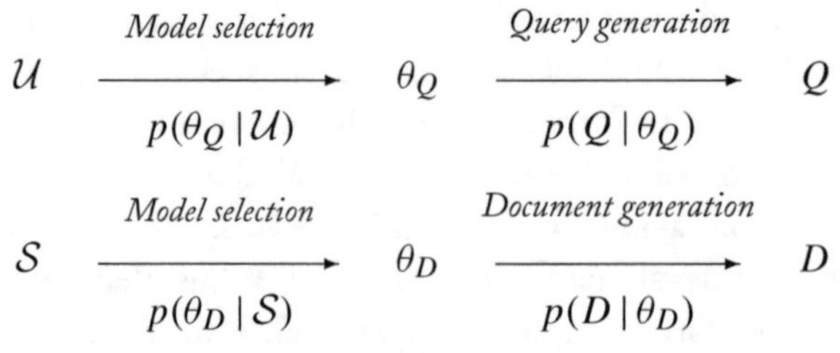

Figure 2.1: Generative model of query Q and document D (from [1]).

Suppose $C = \{D_1, D_2, \ldots, D_N\}$ is a collection of documents obtained from sources $\vec{S} = (S_1, \ldots, S_N)$. The complete set of observed variables would be $\{U, Q, \vec{S}, C\}$. The main idea of the risk minimization framework is to regard the retrieval problem as for the system to choose an optimal *retrieval action* in response to these observations.

A retrieval action is defined generally as a *compound decision* involving *selecting* a subset of documents D from C and *presenting* them to the user who has issued query Q according to some presentation strategy π. We can represent all actions by $A = \{(D_i, \pi_i)\}$, where $D_i \subseteq C$ is a subset of C (results) and π_i is a presentation strategy.

In the general framework of Bayesian decision theory, to each such action $a_i = (D_i, \pi_i) \in A$ there is associated a *loss* $L(a_i, \theta, F(U), F(\vec{S}))$, which in general depends upon all of the parameters of our model $\theta \equiv (\theta_Q, \{\theta_i\}_{i=1}^N)$ as well as any relevant user factors $F(U)$ and document source factors $F(\vec{S})$.

In this framework, the *expected risk of action a_i* is given by

$$R(D_i, \pi_i \,|\, U, Q, \vec{S}, C) \;=\; \int_{\Theta} L(D_i, \pi_i, \theta, F(U), F(\vec{S}))\, p(\theta \,|\, U, Q, \vec{S}, C)\, d\theta \,,$$

where the posterior distribution is given by

$$p(\theta \,|\, U, Q, \vec{S}, C) \;\propto\; p(\theta_Q \,|\, Q, U) \prod_{i=1}^{N} p(\theta_i \,|\, D_i, \vec{S}) \,.$$

The Bayes decision rule is then to choose the action $\mathbf{a}^*$ with the least expected risk:

$$\mathbf{a}^* \;=\; (D^*, \pi^*) \;=\; \underset{D, \pi}{\arg\min}\, R(D, \pi \,|\, U, Q, \vec{S}, C) \,.$$

That is, to select D^* and present D^* with strategy π^*.

Conceptually, this is indeed a very general formulation of retrieval as a decision problem, which involves searching for D^* and π^* simultaneously. The presentation strategy can be fairly arbitrary in principle, e.g., presenting documents in a certain order, presenting a summary of the documents, or presenting a clustering view of the documents. Documents and queries can also be modeled generally with statistical language models. Practically, however, in order to obtain an operational retrieval function that can be computed, we need to quantify the loss associated with a presentation strategy and precisely define the exact language models for documents and queries.

The use of language models in the risk minimization framework makes the framework quite different from other general retrieval frameworks such as the inference network; in particular, it makes the framework more *operational*. Indeed, an operational document ranking formula can always be derived by specifying three components: (1) The query model $p(Q \,|\, \theta_Q)$ and $p(\theta_Q \,|\, U)$; (2) The document model $p(D \,|\, \theta_D)$ and $p(\theta_D \,|\, S)$; (3) The loss function. A different specification of these components leads to a different operational model.

In [89] and [90], many special cases of loss functions and language models are studied, and the risk minimization framework is shown to be able to not only cover most existing retrieval models as special cases, but also conveniently model some novel retrieval problems such as subtopic retrieval [91], which requires going beyond independent relevance, an assumption made in virtually all the traditional models. The framework is also shown to serve well as a road map for systematically exploring the use of language models in information retrieval.

It is worth mentioning that the Generative Relevance Framework proposed by Lavrenko in [92] can also be regarded as a special case of the risk minimization framework. The generative relevance framework is based on the following hypothesis.

Generative Relevance Hypothesis: For a given information need, queries expressing that need and documents relevant to that need can be viewed as independent random samples from the same underlying generative model.

Lavrenko developed three different retrieval functions under this hypothesis (i.e., query likelihood, document likelihood, and KL-divergence) and proposed a general technique called kernel-based allocation for estimating various kinds of language models [92].

The generative relevance hypothesis has two important implications from the perspective of deriving retrieval models: (1) It naturally accommodates matching of queries and documents even if they are in different languages (as in the case of cross-lingual retrieval) or in different media (e.g., text queries on images). (2) It makes it possible to estimate and improve a relevant *document* language model based on examples of *queries* and vice versa.

Conceptually, the generative relevance framework can be regarded as a special case of risk minimization when document models and query models are assumed to be in the same space. Specifically, let $\Theta' = \{(\theta_Q, \theta_D)\}$ be the set of models in the cross-product space of the "natural" query model and "natural" document model which we would normally use in the risk minimization framework. We can define a new query model θ'_Q and a new document model θ'_D both as a model in this new model space Θ'. That is, $\theta'_Q, \theta'_D \in \Theta'$. We can now regard a query Q as a sample of θ'_Q in the sense that $p(Q|\theta'_Q) = p(Q|(\theta_Q, \theta_D)) = p(Q|\theta_Q)$. Similarly, we can view a document D as a sample of θ'_D and have $p(D|\theta'_D) = p(D|(\theta_Q, \theta_D)) = p(D|\theta_D)$. We thus see that both Q and D can be regarded as samples from the same generative model (θ_Q, θ_D).

Before the risk minimization framework, decision-theoretic analysis was applied to choose and weight indexing terms [30, 29, 93], and to justify the probability ranking principle [50], but the action/decision space considered there was limited to a binary decision regarding whether to retrieve a document or regarding whether to assign an index term to a document. The risk minimization framework adopts a much more general action space, which, in principle, consists of all the possible actions that the system can take in response to a query.

The general decision-theoretic view of retrieval adopted in the risk minimization framework makes it possible to model an interactive retrieval process as a sequential decision process, where the user variable $\mathcal{U}$ changes over time. Indeed, if we allow the system to accept any user response, rather than just a text query, as input, then the framework would be able to go beyond search and serve as a formal framework for a general interactive information access system.

2.6   SUMMARY

There is a large body of literature on the study of information retrieval models. The central research question is how to rank text documents in response to a text query optimally so that highly relevant documents would be ranked higher than the less relevant ones. Most work so far is based on the simple bag-of-words representation of text, though it can also be generalized to handle a representation based on larger units such as phrases.

Although in many applications there are also other noncontent features (e.g., links on the Web) that can be exploited to improve ranking accuracy, content-based matching remains the most important component in any search engine, and its performance can significantly affect the overall utility of a search engine.

Over the decades, many different retrieval models have been proposed. However, interestingly, empirically effective models seem to all boil down to some form of implementation of the three major retrieval heuristics (i.e., TF, IDF, and document length normalization), and when optimized, these different models tend to all perform similarly well. In other words, the clear difference in how these models are motivated or derived does not seem to matter that much as the subtle difference in how exactly they implement these retrieval heuristics. Thus, although much research has been done in seeking an optimal retrieval model, it is fair to say that it remains a significant challenge in information retrieval research to develop a model that is both theoretically sound and able to perform well empirically. We do not yet have a clear single winner among all the models that can consistently outperform all other models.

Before the language modeling approaches were proposed, the two most effective retrieval functions were the pivoted length normalization function [46] and the BM25 function [70]; both functions are based on TF-IDF weighting and document length normalization. The main feedback methods for these retrieval functions are Rocchio [34] for the vector space model and the Offer Weight method for term selection in probabilistic models [67]. The development of language modeling approaches has resulted in another effective retrieval function—the query likelihood language modeling retrieval function (with appropriate smoothing) [74, 94]. The most effective feedback methods for the language modeling approaches are mostly based on the KL-divergence retrieval function [1], which can be regarded as a generalization of the query likelihood retrieval function. In the following chapters of the book, we will systematically introduce these language modeling approaches to retrieval.

To avoid confusion, it is worth adding a brief discussion about the term "language modeling approach." Generally speaking, any retrieval model involving the use of a probabilistic model of text can be referred to as a language modeling approach. In particular, the classical probabilistic retrieval models such as the binary independence model can also be regarded as instances of language modeling approaches with document modeled by a multiple Bernoulli language model. However, for historical reasons, the term often only refers to either the use of n-gram language models (e.g., unigram and bigram language models) or the query likelihood retrieval function and its generalization, the KL-divergence retrieval model. Recently, the term seems to have been used more and more liberally to refer to any retrieval model in which a probabilistic model of text is involved, though. In this book, we will use the term "language modeling approach" mainly in its narrow sense so as to be consistent with how the term has been used in most of the existing literature. Regardless how we define the term, our philosophy is to emphasize more on probabilistic models that are either empirically effective or theoretically important.

CHAPTER 3

Simple Query Likelihood Retrieval Model

The language modeling approach (in its narrow definition) was first introduced by Ponte and Croft in their SIGIR 98 paper [74]. In this work, they proposed a new way to score a document, later often called the *query likelihood* scoring method. Since then, the query likelihood retrieval model has become the basic language modeling approach. In this chapter, we introduce the simple query likelihood retrieval model, which represents the very first generation of language models applied to information retrieval. These models are as effective as the traditional retrieval models and also have similar computational complexity, making them excellent alternatives to the traditional TF-IDF weighting retrieval functions. Extensions of the simple query likelihood retrieval models have led to more effective, but computationally more complex query likelihood retrieval models; they will be discussed in the next chapter.

3.1 BASIC IDEA

The basic idea of the query likelihood retrieval model is rather simple: We assume that a query is a sample drawn from a language model. To score a document, we would first estimate a language model for the document, and then compute the likelihood of the query according to the estimated language model. We can then rank all the documents based on their query likelihood scores.

Formally, let Q be a query and D a document. Let θ_D be a language model estimated based on document D. The score of document D w.r.t. query Q is then defined as the conditional probability $p(Q|\theta_D)$. That is,

$$score(D, Q) = p(Q|\theta_D) .$$

One immediate question is: how should we interpret the document language model θ_D? What does it model? The derivation of the query-generation probabilistic models in Chapter 2 shows that $p(Q|\theta_D)$ should really be interpreted as $p(Q|D, R = r)$, i.e., the probability that a user who likes document D would use query Q (to retrieve the document). Thus, θ_D should be interpreted as modeling the queries that a user would use in order to retrieve document D. That is, although the θ_D in the query likelihood scoring formula is often called a document language model, it is really a model for queries, not documents.

Intuitively, given a query Q, the query likelihood retrieval model would test each document D to see whether a user would likely use the current query Q to retrieve D if the user likes document D, and rank the documents based on this query likelihood. In an extreme case, imagine that all users who like document D would always use query Q to retrieve D, we would have $p(Q|\theta_D) = 1$. Thus, if we see query Q again, we would rank D on the top because it has the highest query likelihood, which makes sense. On the other hand, if a user who wants to retrieve document D would never use query Q, we would have $p(Q|\theta_D) = 0$. Thus, we would rank this document at the bottom for query Q, which again makes sense.

Clearly, in order to estimate θ_D, ideally we should use many actual queries used by users who want to retrieve document D. For example, we may assume that if a user clicks on a web page in search results, he/she likes the document. Under this assumption, we can use all the queries of the users who clicked on document D to estimate θ_D. However, in reality, only very few documents get clicked on and certainly there are always queries that we would not even have seen. Yet, as a general retrieval model, the query likelihood retrieval model must have some way to score any document with respect to any query. The solution to this problem taken by the simple query likelihood retrieval model is to simply estimate θ_D based on D, i.e., we would use document D to approximate the queries that a user would use to retrieve D. It is easy to see that with this approximation, the query likelihood retrieval model would generally reward a document that matches many query terms many times because in such a case, the estimated θ_D would tend to have high probabilities for query terms (since they occur many times in the document), thus it will give the query a high probability.

Clearly, in order to use such a model to score documents, we must solve two problems: (1) What probabilistic model should we use to define θ_D? (2) How can we estimate θ_D? Thus, with the query likelihood retrieval model, the retrieval problem essentially boils down to answering these two questions. In the following section, we will present several specific models of θ_D and discuss how to estimate them.

3.2   EVENT MODELS FOR θ_D

Since θ_D is to model queries, in general, it can be any language model. However, the choice of a specific model can affect retrieval performance significantly. The two important factors to be considered when deciding how to instantiate θ_D are: (1) Are the assumptions made by the model reasonable for the retrieval task being considered? (2) Can we estimate the model parameters reliably?

So far, using a unigram multinomial language model for θ_D has been most popular and most successful. However, other choices are also possible. For example, multiple Bernoulli was used in Ponte and Croft's work [74] when they first introduced the query likelihood retrieval model. Poisson is another possibility explored recently [95]. We now discuss these choices in more detail.

3.2.1   MULTINOMIAL θ_D

Assuming a multinomial language model, we would generate a sequence of words by generating each word independently. Thus, a multinomial model θ_D would have the same number of parameters (i.e., word probabilities) as the number of words in our vocabulary set V, i.e., $\{p(w_i|\theta_D)\}_{i=1}^{|V|}$. Clearly, we have $\sum_{i=1}^{|V|} p(w|\theta_D) = 1$.

Now suppose $Q = q_1...q_m$. The query likelihood would be

$$
\begin{aligned}
p(Q|\theta_D) &= \prod_{i=1}^{m} p(q_i|\theta_D) \\
&= \prod_{w \in V} p(w|\theta_D)^{c(w,Q)} ,
\end{aligned}
$$

where $c(w, Q)$ is the count of word w in query Q.

With such a model, the retrieval problem is reduced to the problem of estimating $p(w_i|\theta_D)$.

3.2.2 MULTIPLE BERNOULLI θ_D

When using a multiple Bernoulli model, we define a binary random variable $X_i \in \{0, 1\}$ for each word w_i to indicate whether word w_i is present ($X_i = 1$) or absent ($X_i = 0$) in the query. We assume that the presence or absence of each word is independent of each other. Thus, a multiple Bernoulli model θ_D would again have the same number of parameters as the number of words in the vocabulary, i.e., $\theta_D = \{p(X_i = 1|\theta_D)\}_{i=1}^{|V|}$. Such a model can model presence and absence of words in the query, and our constraints are $p(X_i = 1|\theta_D) + p(X_i = 0|\theta_D) = 1$ for $i = 1, ..., |V|$. Note the difference between these constraints and those for the multinomial distribution.

According to the multiple Bernoulli model, the query likelihood would be:

$$
p(Q|\theta_D) = \prod_{w_i \in Q} p(X_i = 1|\theta_D) \prod_{w_j \notin Q} (1 - p(X_j = 1|\theta_D)) ,
$$

where the first product is for words in the query, and the second for words not occurring in the query.

The retrieval problem has now been reduced to the problem of estimating $p(X_i = 1|\theta_D)$.

3.2.3 MULTIPLE POISSON θ_D

When using a multiple Poisson model, we define a Poisson random variable $X_i \in \{0\} \cup \aleph$ for each word w_i to model the frequency of word w_i in the query. We model the frequency of each word independently. As in the case of multinomial and multiple Bernoulli, the multiple Poisson model θ_D also has the same number of parameters as the number of words in our vocabulary, i.e., $\theta_D = \{\lambda_i\}_{i=1}^{|V|}$, where λ_i is the mean rate of a Poisson process corresponding to X_i.

According to the Poisson distribution, the probability of observing x counts of a word during time period t from a Poisson process with parameter λ is

$$
p(X = x|\lambda) = \frac{e^{-\lambda t}(\lambda t)^x}{x!} .
$$

To model the counts of a word in the query, we take the query length m as the length of the time period. Thus, the query likelihood is:

$$
p(Q|\theta_D) = \prod_{w_i \in V} \frac{e^{-\lambda_i m}(\lambda_i m)^{c(w_i,Q)}}{c(w_i, Q)!} .
$$

The retrieval problem has now been reduced to the problem of estimating λ_i.

3.2.4   COMPARISON OF THE THREE MODELS

The three models presented above make different assumptions about word occurrences. The multinomial model assumes that every occurrence of a word, including the multiple occurrences of the same word, is independent. The multiple Bernoulli model assumes that the occurrences of different words are independent. Compared with the multinomial model, the multiple Bernoulli model makes a weaker independence assumption, but this is at the price of not being able to model multiple occurrences. The multiple Poisson model is similar to multiple Bernoulli in that each word is modeled through an independent model, which naturally offers flexibility in estimating the parameters for different words in different ways; in this aspect, they are different from multinomial model[1]. However, the Poisson model has an advantage over Bernoulli in capturing term frequencies.

Most research so far has focused on the multinomial model, even though multiple Bernoulli was the model used in the pioneering work by Ponte and Croft [74]. When each word in a document is regarded as a sample of multiple Bernoulli where only this word has shown up, but all other words have not, it can be shown that estimation of multiple Bernoulli is related to the estimation of the multinomial model [96]. Empirically, there has been some evidence that multinomial outperforms multiple Bernoulli [97], but a more systematic comparison between them is needed in order to draw definitive conclusions[2]. Poisson model appears to have some advantages [95], but there has not been much work on this model yet.

3.3   ESTIMATION OF θ_D

Since most existing work is on the multinomial model, we will only discuss the estimation of θ_D for the multinomial model. Estimation of multiple Bernoulli model and multiple Poisson model can be found in the related research work [74] and [95].

Recall that θ_D models what kind of queries would be posed by users who like document D. Without assuming the availability of any examples of such queries, we use D as an approximation. That is, we assume that D is a sample of θ_D. Thus, according to the maximum likelihood (ML) estimator, we have (see Section 1.2):

$$p_{ml}(w|\theta_D) = \frac{c(w, D)}{\sum_{w \in V} c(w, D)} = \frac{c(w, D)}{|D|} .$$

One problem with this ML estimator is that an unseen word in document D would get a zero probability, making all queries containing an unseen word have zero probability for the entire query $p(Q|\theta_D)$. This is clearly undesirable.

More importantly, since a document is a very small sample for our model, the ML estimate is generally not accurate, so an important problem we have to solve is to *smooth* the ML estimator so

---

[1]Although one can also potentially introduce this flexibility into a multinomial model through Bayesian estimation and using word-specific parameters in a prior, it is not as natural as in multiple Poisson or multiple Bernoulli.
[2]The two event models are also compared in [66] for text categorization.

that we do not assign zero probability to unseen words and improve the accuracy of the estimated language model in general. Smoothing has been shown to play a critical role in the query likelihood retrieval model [98]; it plays a similar role to term weighting in a traditional model.

In order to assign nonzero probabilities to unseen words, we will have to discount the probabilities of the observed words in D so that we will have some extra probability mass for the unseen words. There are many different ways of smoothing an ML estimator. The simplest way to smooth the ML estimator $p_{ml}(w|\theta_D)$ is to assume that each word, including an unseen word, has got a small amount of extra count ϵ, thus an unseen word would have a nonzero count:

$$p_\epsilon(w|\hat{\theta}_D) = \frac{c(w, D) + \epsilon}{|D| + \epsilon|V|}$$

where $\epsilon > 0$ is a smoothing parameter.

This method is called *additive smoothing* [99]; the special case of $\epsilon = 1$ is called Laplace smoothing. When $\epsilon = 0$, we recover the original ML estimate (i.e., no smoothing).

The additive smoothing method gives all the unseen words the same probability (i.e., $\epsilon/(|D| + \epsilon|V|)$). Is this reasonable? Intuitively, a word like "unicorn" should probably have a smaller probability than "animal" even though none of them occurred in a document. Thus, a more reasonable smoothing method should give different unseen words potentially different probabilities. However, based on what should we determine which unseen word has a higher probability? In general, we may assume that the probability of an unseen word is proportional to the probability of the word given by a reference language model. For information retrieval, a natural choice of the reference language model would be the language model estimated based on the entire document collection, called a *collection language model* or a *background language model*, since intuitively it reflects the general word frequencies in the collection. We now discuss this general smoothing strategy in detail.

3.3.1 A GENERAL SMOOTHING STRATEGY USING COLLECTION LANGUAGE MODEL

We first discuss how to estimate a collection language model, which is also referred to a background language model or a reference language model.

Let $p(w|C)$ denote the collection language model. Intuitively, we can estimate it by normalizing the counts of words in the entire collection, but there are some variations as to how exactly we normalize these counts. One popular way is to estimate it as:

$$p(w|C) = \frac{\sum_{D \in C} c(w, D)}{\sum_{D \in C} |D|}.$$

Alternatively, we can estimate it as

$$p(w|C) = \frac{1}{|C|} \sum_{D \in C} \frac{c(w, D)}{|D|}.$$

The difference is that in the first equation, we assume that each *word* contributes equally while in the second, each *document* contributes equally. Which method is a better choice would depend on which of these two assumptions makes more sense. Most research work has assumed the first equation.

Yet another alternative is to ignore the actual frequency of a word in a document and simply obtain the estimate by counting how many documents contain a word and normalizing the counts [100]:

$$p(w|C) = \frac{\sum_{D \in C} \delta(w, D)}{\sum_{w \in V} \sum_{D \in C} \delta(w, D)}$$

where $\delta(w, D) = 1$ if word w occurs in document D, and otherwise $\delta(w, D) = 0$.

Because the collection is usually large, the differences between these alternative strategies tend to be insignificant. But it is still a very interesting research direction to compare these different strategies systematically.

Given our definition of the collection language model, we can define a smoothed language model generally as

$$p(w|\hat{\theta}_D) = \begin{cases} p_s(w|\theta_D) & \text{if word } w \text{ is seen in } D \\ \alpha_D \, p(w|C) & \text{otherwise}, \end{cases} \tag{3.1}$$

where $p_s(w|\theta_D)$ is the smoothed probability of a word seen in document D and α_D is a coefficient controlling the probability mass assigned to unseen words.

In general, α_D may depend on D, and if $p_s(w|\theta_D)$ is given, we must have

$$\alpha_D = \frac{1 - \sum_{w \in V : c(w; D) > 0} p_s(w|\theta_D)}{1 - \sum_{w \in V : c(w; D) > 0} p(w|C)} \tag{3.2}$$

to ensure that all probabilities sum to one. In this sense, individual smoothing methods can be regarded as essentially differing in their choice of $p_s(w|\theta_D)$.

We now discuss several special cases of this general smoothing scheme.

3.3.2   JELINEK-MERCER SMOOTHING (FIXED COEFFICIENT INTERPOLATION)

In this method, we interpolate the maximum likelihood estimate with the collection language model with a fixed coefficient λ to control the amount of smoothing:

$$p_\lambda(w|\hat{\theta}_D) = (1 - \lambda)\frac{c(w, D)}{|D|} + \lambda p(w|C) \,.$$

Clearly, when $\lambda = 0$, we end up having the original ML estimate, while if $\lambda = 1$, all the θ_D's would become the same as the collection language model $p(w|C)$. In this method, $\alpha_D = \lambda$; every document has the same amount of smoothing.

3.3.3   DIRICHLET PRIOR SMOOTHING

In this smoothing method, we use a Bayesian estimator instead of the ML estimator to estimate θ_D. As explained in Section 1.2, an advantage of Bayesian estimation over ML estimation is that we can impose a prior on the parameter so that the estimated parameter value would not only fit the data well but also be consistent with our prior.

For estimating θ_D, our prior would encode our belief that it should not assign a zero-probability to many words. In fact, when we use the collection language model for smoothing, we could have a prior to prefer a θ_D that is close to the collection language model. As we will see, such a prior essentially would add extra pseudo counts for all the words; a word with a higher probability according to the collection language model would have a higher pseudo count. As a result, when we pool these pseudo counts with the actual counts of words observed in the document, we would effectively combine our prior with the data to estimate the probability of each word.

Formally, we may use a Dirichlet prior on θ_D with parameters $\alpha = (\alpha_1, \alpha_2, \ldots, \alpha_{|V|})$, given by

$$\mathrm{Dir}\,(\theta \mid \alpha) \;=\; \frac{\Gamma(\sum_{i=1}^{|V|} \alpha_i)}{\prod_{i=1}^{|V|} \Gamma(\alpha_i)} \prod_{i=1}^{|V|} \theta_i^{\alpha_i - 1} \tag{3.3}$$

where Γ is the gamma function (an extension of the factorial function to real and complex numbers). The parameters α_i are chosen to be $\alpha_i = \mu\, p(w_i \mid C)$ where μ is a parameter and $p(\cdot \mid C)$ is the collection language model.

Dirichlet is a conjugate prior for multinomial, which essentially means that the prior distribution is of a similar functional form to that of the likelihood function, thus allowing us to "convert" the prior into "pseudo data" to be pooled together with the observed data. Indeed, with the Dirichlet prior, the posterior distribution of θ_D is given by

$$p(\theta_D \mid D) \;\propto\; \prod_{w \in V} p(w \mid \theta_D)^{c(w,D) + \mu p(w \mid C) - 1}$$

and so is also Dirichlet, with parameters $\alpha_i = c(w_i, D) + \mu p(w_i \mid C)$.

Using the fact that the Dirichlet mean is $\alpha_j / \sum_k \alpha_k$, we have that

$$\begin{aligned} p_\mu(w \mid \hat{\theta}_D) &= \int_{\theta_D} p(w \mid \theta_D) p(\theta_D \mid D) d\theta_D \\ &= \frac{c(w, D) + \mu\, p(w \mid C)}{|D| + \mu}. \end{aligned}$$

It is easy to see that the Dirichlet prior smoothing method also interpolates the ML estimate with the collection language model, but with a *dynamic* coefficient that changes according to the document length:

$$p_\mu(w \mid \hat{\theta}_D) = \frac{|D|}{|D| + \mu} \frac{c(w, D)}{|D|} + \frac{\mu}{\mu + |D|} p(w \mid C)\,.$$

Comparing this with Jelinek-Mercer smoothing, we are essentially setting $\lambda = \frac{\mu}{\mu+|D|}$. For a fixed μ, this means that a longer document will get less smoothing, which makes sense since a longer document is a larger sample, thus would need less smoothing. Indeed, as $|D| \to \infty$, there will be no smoothing and we simply recover the ML estimate. Such a phenomenon of "eventually data overriding prior" is a general property of a Bayesian estimator.

The Dirichlet prior smoothing method adds a pseudo count $\mu p(w|C)$ to each word. Thus, the additive smoothing method can be regarded as a special case of Dirichlet prior smoothing with a uniform collection language model.

3.3.4 ABSOLUTE DISCOUNTING SMOOTHING

The idea of the absolute discounting method is to lower the probability of seen words by subtracting a constant from their counts [101]. It is similar to the Jelinek-Mercer method, but differs in that it discounts the seen word probability by subtracting a constant instead of multiplying it by $(1-\lambda)$. The model is given by

$$p_\delta(w \mid \hat{\theta}_D) = \frac{\max(c(w, D) - \delta, 0)}{\sum_{w' \in V} c(w', D)} + \sigma p(w \mid C) \tag{3.4}$$

where $\delta \in [0, 1]$ is a discount constant and $\sigma = \delta |D|_u / |D|$, so that all probabilities sum to one. Here, $|D|_u$ is the number of *unique* terms in document D, and $|D|$ is the total count of words in the document, so that $|D| = \sum_{w' \in V} c(w', D)$.

3.3.5 INTERPOLATION VS. BACKOFF

One may note that in the three smoothing methods discussed above, we discount the counts of the seen words (which is why we can assign nonzero probabilities to unseen words), but the extra counts are *shared* by both the seen words and unseen words. Mathematically, it is seen that all these smoothing formulas involve an interpolation of the collection language model with a variant of the original ML estimate.

One problem of this approach is that a high count word may actually end up with more than its actual count in the document, if it is frequent according to the reference (collection) model. This may not be reasonable because intuitively, if we have already observed many occurrences of a word in the document, the maximum likelihood estimate for that word is relatively reliable.

An alternative smoothing strategy is "backoff." Here, the main idea is to trust the maximum likelihood estimate for high count words, and to discount and redistribute mass only for the less common terms. As a result, it differs from the interpolation strategy in that the extra counts are primarily used for unseen words. The Katz smoothing method is a well-known backoff method [102]. The backoff strategy is very popular and useful in speech recognition tasks.

For retrieval, however, such a backoff strategy is ineffective [98] because smoothing also serves for the purpose of discriminating query words (i.e., achieving an effect of IDF), and interpolation is needed to achieve this discrimination effect. This second role of smoothing for achieving IDF effect will be further discussed in detail in Section 3.4. Although backoff alone is not effective [98], combining backoff with interpolation may be a reasonable strategy, but this has not yet been studied.

3.3.6 OTHER SMOOTHING METHODS

There are many other smoothing methods that can be potentially used for estimating θ_D (see, e.g., [99]). Here we mention one of them: Good-Turing.

The idea of Good-Turing smoothing [103] is to assume that the total number of unseen events is equal to the total number of singletons (i.e., words occurring once) and adjust the counts of all the seen events in this way. We can then use the adjusted count of a word to estimate its probability.

Formally, let $\hat{c}(w, d)$ be the adjusted count of word w, we have:

$$p(w|\hat{\theta}_D) = \frac{\hat{c}(w, D)}{|D|} .$$

Let n_r denote the number of words occurring precisely r times in D. The adjustment of counts is performed through the following equation:

$$\hat{c}(w, D)n_{c(w,D)} = (c(w, D) + 1)n_{c(w,D)+1} .$$

That is, we want the total adjusted counts of all words occurring $c(w, D)$ times (the left side) to be equal to the total real counts of all words occurring $c(w, D) + 1$ times (right side). Thus, we have:

$$\hat{0} = \frac{n_1}{n_0}, \quad \hat{1} = \frac{2n_2}{n_1}, \quad \dots ,$$

where n_0 is the total number of unseen words.

Intuitively, this can be understood as pretending that none of the singletons had ever been observed, thus we can use the total number of singleton occurrences (the same as the number of distinct singletons) to estimate the total occurrences of unseen words. Such a strategy can be justified based on leave-one-out cross validation [14].

One challenge to be solved with Good-Turing is how to handle the case when $n_r = 0$ for some r. Techniques such as interpolation have been proposed to address this problem [104]. Note that in Good-Turing we have not used the reference language model $p(w|C)$, but it is not hard to add it so that the probability of an unseen word is proportional to $p(w|C)$ as we have seen in some other smoothing methods. As in the case of backoff, we may also need to further interpolate Good-Turing with $p(w|C)$ to help discriminating query words.

3.3.7 COMPARISON OF DIFFERENT SMOOTHING METHODS

In the query likelihood retrieval model, the retrieval function mainly varies in how smoothing is done when we estimate θ_D. Given that there are many different ways of smoothing, it is not surprising that retrieval accuracy is quite sensitive to the choice of smoothing method and the setting of a smoothing parameter. In [98], a systematic study of three different smoothing methods

(Jelinek-Mercer, Dirichlet prior, and absolute discounting) has been conducted. It was found that: (1) interpolation-based smoothing strategies work better than backoff strategies; (2) Dirichlet prior smoothing appears to work the best among all the methods tested. Dirichlet prior smoothing has now been widely recognized as one of the most effective smoothing methods for retrieval.

The study has also revealed that the sensitivity pattern of performance to smoothing varies according to query types, which suggests that smoothing is needed for two quite different purposes in the query likelihood retrieval model: (1) it is needed to compensate for the small sample problem (a document is a small sample); (2) it is needed to model the noise in the query and help discriminating query words (in effect achieving IDF term weighting). This is called the dual role of smoothing, an issue we will further discuss in the next subsection.

3.4   SMOOTHING AND TF-IDF WEIGHTING

There is some interesting connection between the use of a collection language model for smoothing in the query likelihood retrieval model and the TF-IDF weighting heuristics used in a traditional retrieval model, which may partly explain why query likelihood is an effective retrieval model. This connection appears to be first derived in [75, 105] for the fixed interpolation smoothing method. In [94], a more general connection is derived for a family of smoothing methods. We now explain this derivation in detail.

Assuming the general smoothing scheme presented in Section 3.3, we can rewrite the query likelihood retrieval function as follows (we will actually work with log-likelihood which does not affect ranking of documents):

$$
\begin{aligned}
\log p(Q|\theta_D) &= \sum_{w \in V} c(w, Q) \log p(w|\theta_D) \\
&= \sum_{w \in D} c(w, Q) \log p_s(w|\theta_D) + \sum_{w \notin D} c(w, Q) \log \alpha_D p(w|C) \\
&= \sum_{w \in D} c(w, Q) \log p_s(w|\theta_D) + \sum_{w \in V} c(w, Q) \log \alpha_D p(w|C) - \sum_{w \in D} c(w, Q) \log \alpha_D p(w|C) .
\end{aligned}
$$

Note that we have rewritten the sum over all the missing query words in D as the difference between a sum over all the query words and a sum over the query words in D. This is a commonly used technique to convert a sum not easy to compute to sums that are easier to compute in probabilistic models.

By grouping the first and third terms (both are sums over the words occurring in D), we have:

$$
\log p(Q|\theta_D) = \sum_{w \in D} c(w, Q) \log \frac{p_s(w|\theta_D)}{\alpha_D p(w|C)} + |Q| \log \alpha_D + \sum_{w \in V} c(w, Q) \log p(w|C) .
$$

We further notice that we can ignore the last term because it does not affect ranking of documents. Thus, we have the following query likelihood ranking formula:

$$\log p(Q|\theta_D) \stackrel{\text{rank}}{=} \sum_{w \in D} c(w, Q) \log \frac{p_s(w|\theta_D)}{\alpha_D \, p(w|C)} + |Q| \log \alpha_D . \tag{3.5}$$

This rewriting reveals interesting *general* connections between the query likelihood retrieval functions and traditional retrieval functions such as pivoted length normalization and BM25 [26] when the document language model is smoothed with the collection language model:

First, the form of the retrieval function is similar; indeed, the query likelihood retrieval function also involves a sum over all the matched query terms (i.e., terms for which $c(w, Q) > 0$ and $c(w, D) > 0$). Since the second term can be precomputed easily, this means that the query likelihood retrieval function can be computed as efficiently as any existing retrieval model, and the inverted index can be leveraged to speed up the computation.

Second, each matched query term contributes a weight reflecting TF-IDF weighting. The weight of a matched term w can be identified as the logarithm of $\frac{p_s(w|\theta_D)}{\alpha_D \, p(w|C)}$, which is essentially similar to TF-IDF weighting. Indeed, $p_s(w|\theta_D)$ would be larger for a term occurring more frequently in document D, so the weight of such a term would be higher (TF heuristic). Also, a frequent term in the collection would have a high $p(w|C)$, thus a smaller overall weight. This means that popular terms would get penalized (IDF heuristic). Document length normalization is done through two terms: (1) the estimate of $p_s(w|\theta_D)$ generally involves length normalization, and for the same count of words, this probability would be smaller for a longer document, thus penalizing long documents. (2) α_D is presumably related to document length because a shorter document is expected to require more smoothing thus a larger α_D. But since the two occurrences of α_D in the formula have opposite effect, it has mixed effect on length normalization.

This analysis reveals another important fact: the IDF weighting in the query likelihood retrieval model is achieved *indirectly* through smoothing with the collection language model $p(w|C)$. This is indeed a very important point as it suggests that smoothing plays two roles in this retrieval function: (1) estimation improvement: it helps improve our estimate of θ_D when D is small; (2) query term discrimination (IDF): it helps down-weighting common terms in the query through modeling the noise in a query with the collection language model; a word with a high probability according to $p(w|C)$ would be penalized. This also means that if we have a good model for what kind of terms in the query *should* be penalized, we should smooth the document language models with such a query noisy model so that we can effectively penalize the noisy terms.

The following example illustrates how smoothing with a background language model can achieve query term discrimination. Suppose we have a query "algorithms for data mining," and the unsmoothed ML estimate of two document language models is shown in Table 3.1. Intuitively, D_2 should be ranked higher than D_1 because it matches the content query words (i.e., "data", "mining", and "algorithms") better. However, if we use these unsmoothed language models to compute the query likelihood, we will see that $p(Q|D_1) > p(Q|D_2)$ because D_1 has a much higher probability for the common word "for."

Now suppose we perform Jelinek-Mercer smoothing with $\lambda = 0.9$ and with the collection language model shown in the same table. We will obtain the smoothed language models shown in the last two rows in the table. It is easy to see that after smoothing, $p(Q|D_2) > p(Q|D_1)$ as desired! What happens is that because the collection language model gives "for" a much higher probability, after smoothing, each document would have a very high probability for "for," in effect, this reduces or eliminates any original difference between the probabilities of "for" given by the ML estimates of the two documents. On the other hand, the content words all have very small probabilities according to $p(w|C)$, thus smoothing does not really help on such words, allowing the original differences on such words to "survive" smoothing and make significant contributions to the overall scores.

Table 3.1: Illustration of smoothing for query term discrimination					
Query		algorithms	for	data	mining
Unsmoothed	$p_{ml}(w|\theta_{D_1})$	0.001	0.025	0.002	0.003
	$p_{ml}(w|\theta_{D_2})$	0.001	0.01	0.003	0.004
CollectLM	$p(w|C)$	0.00001	0.2	0.00001	0.00001
Smoothed	$p(w|\theta_{D_1})$	0.000109	0.1825	0.000209	0.000309
	$p(w|\theta_{D_2})$	0.000109	0.181	0.000309	0.000409

The analysis of the dual role of smoothing also suggests that even if our documents are extremely long (thus the ML estimate is accurate), we may still need smoothing for the IDF purpose. It also provides a possible explanation why effective smoothing strategies for speech recognition such as backoff alone do not perform well for retrieval; they cannot fulfill the second role well.

3.5   TWO-STAGE SMOOTHING

The dual role of smoothing suggests that it may be a good idea to implement the two roles separately rather than relying on a single smoothing method to achieve both goals. Experiment results in [98] suggest that Dirichlet prior smoothing works the best for fulfilling the first role while the Jelinek-Mercer smoothing method is most effective for fulfilling the second role. Intuitively, this also makes sense because for improving the estimate of θ_D, it makes sense to use a *dynamic* coefficient as in Dirichlet prior smoothing so that a longer document would have less smoothing, whereas for query term discrimination, we should use a *fixed* coefficient for interpolation, or otherwise the degree of query term discrimination would vary from document to document, which is unreasonable.

Thus, we can combine Dirichlet prior with Jelinek-Mercer to obtain a two-stage smoothing method [109]: given the ML estimate of θ_D, we would first smooth it with Dirichlet prior (to address the small sample problem) and then further smooth it by interpolating the language model with another language model for modeling noise in the query $p(w|Noise)$. Formally, the final smoothed language model is given by:

$$p_{\lambda,\mu}(w|\theta_D) = (1-\lambda)\frac{c(w,D) + \mu p(w|C)}{|D| + \mu} + \lambda p(w|Noise) \,.$$

Without further knowledge, the noise model $p(w|Noise)$ can be assumed to be $p(w|C)$. As discussed earlier, the interpolation with $p(w|C)$ would cause popular terms to have lower weights (essentially implementing the IDF heuristic). Thus, when approximating $p(w|Noise)$ with $p(w|C)$, we essentially add IDF weighting to the retrieval function. This intuitively makes sense because we have assumed that $p(w|C)$ is our noise model (thus a word with high probability $p(w|C)$ should indeed be penalized).

From the viewpoint of a generative model (i.e., interpreting θ_D as $p(Q|D, R = r)$), we may roughly regard $p_{\lambda,\mu}(w|\theta_D)$ as modeling the following generation process of a query given a document: a user who likes document D would formulate a query Q by sampling words from a mixture model with two components, one corresponding to the topic of D and the other general background. With probability λ, the user would generate a background word using $p(w|C)$; with probability $1 - \lambda$, the user would then try to generate a content word. To generate a content word, the user would primarily pick a word from the document, but may also use a word not in the document.

For the second-stage smoothing, the use of the collection language model $p(w|C)$ is reasonable (not necessarily ideal) and would help achieving IDF weighting. However, for the first-stage smoothing, $p(w|C)$ may not be the best. Indeed, ideally we should use additional text closely related to the content of each document to estimate such a reference language model. Such a smoothing strategy has been studied in [106, 107, 2, 108] and can indeed improve retrieval accuracy. But the computation is usually significantly more expensive. We will introduce them in the next chapter.

On the surface, the tuning of two-stage smoothing appears to be harder because it now has two smoothing parameters (instead of just one) to tune. However, in reality, the two parameters are now more meaningful than the one parameter in a single-stage smoothing method. Specifically, μ indicates the amount of smoothing needed to compensate for the small sample problem of a document, thus it can be estimated solely based on the collection of documents without requiring knowledge about the query. λ indicates the amount of noise in the query, which must be estimated after seeing the query. In [109], it was shown that it is possible to use statistical estimation methods to automatically tune these two parameters to achieve near optimal or better performance than well-tuned best performance using single-stage smoothing methods. However, the estimation of λ is computationally expensive, making the approach not so attractive for real-time retrieval applications.

In principle, the two-stage smoothing method is the best simple smoothing method with the same computational complexity as any traditional model. In practice, however, the performance is usually not much better than a well-tuned single stage smoothing method such as Dirichlet prior.

3.6   EXPLOIT DOCUMENT PRIOR

The query likelihood retrieval model can be justified based on the probability ranking principle as we have shown in Section 2.2. In order to justify $p(Q|D, r)$ as a relevance-based ranking function, we have to assume that the document prior $p(r|D)$ is uniform. This is reasonable if we do not have further knowledge about the documents. However, this prior can also be exploited to incorporate any static ranking preferences of documents (i.e., ranking preferences independent of a query) such as PageRank scores or other document features.

Most of the work trying to incorporate such a prior has used the following alternative way to justify the query likelihood retrieval function [76, 110, 75]:

$$p(D|Q) \propto p(Q|D)p(D),$$

where $p(D)$ is regarded as a document prior. While the form is different from what we derived in Section 2.2, the spirit is the same—all attempting to combine some query-independent preferences on documents with the query likelihood score of a document.

In this line of the work, Kraaij et al. [111] successfully leveraged this prior to implement an interesting Web search heuristic for named page finding. Their idea is to prefer pages with shorter URLs since an entry page tends to have a shorter URL. They used some training data to estimate the prior $p(D)$ based on URL lengths, and showed that this prior can improve search performance significantly [111]. Li and Croft [112] studied how to leverage the document prior $p(D)$ to implement time-related preferences in retrieval so that a document with a more recent time would be preferred. This strategy has been shown to be effective for a particular set of "recency queries." In a study by Kurland and Lee [113], a PageRank score computed using induced links between documents based on document similarity has been used as a prior to improve retrieval accuracy. In [114] priors to capture document quality are shown to be effective for improving the accuracy of the top-ranked documents in ad hoc web search.

3.7   SUMMARY

In this chapter, we introduced the simple query likelihood retrieval model, which is roughly characterized by the use of query likelihood for scoring and simple smoothing methods based on a background collection language model. Such a basic language modeling approach (especially with Dirichlet prior smoothing) has been shown to be as effective as well-tuned existing retrieval models such as pivoted length normalization and BM25 [28]. The approach has been quite successfully applied to many different retrieval tasks including, e.g., passage retrieval [115], Web search [111, 116], and genomics retrieval [117], among others. Retrieval functions in this basic language modeling approach can generally be computed as efficiently as any standard TF-IDF retrieval model with the aid of an inverted index; this was shown in [94] through a general transformation of the retrieval function into a form very similar to a TF-IDF retrieval function. The transformation also reveals a general connection between smoothing with a background language model and the IDF heuristic.

While the simple query likelihood retrieval model is efficient to compute and effective, there has been a lot of research on further improving the model. We will review this body of work in the next two chapters.

CHAPTER 4

Complex Query Likelihood Retrieval Model

In Chapter 3, we restricted the discussion to the family of query likelihood retrieval models that use simple smoothing methods based on a background language model. As a result of using simple smoothing methods, their efficiency is comparable to any traditional TF-IDF model. In this chapter, we review some extensions to these simple query likelihood retrieval models. These extensions often outperform, but also tend to be computationally more expensive than the simple models. All these improvements remain in the family of query-likelihood scoring, which distinguishes them from the other models to be reviewed in the next chapter; the latter uses language modeling in a different way than the query likelihood.

4.1 DOCUMENT-SPECIFIC SMOOTHING OF θ_D

Smoothing every document with the *same* collection language model is intuitively not optimal since we essentially assume that all the unseen words in different documents would have similar probabilities. Ideally, we should use some *document-dependent* "augmented text data" that can more accurately reflect the content of the document under consideration. With such reasoning, several researchers have attempted to exploit the corpus structure to achieve such document-specific smoothing.

The work in this line can be grouped into two categories:
(1) Cluster documents and smooth a document with the cluster containing the document.
(2) For each document, obtain the most similar documents in the collection and then smooth the document with the obtained "neighbor documents."

4.1.1 CLUSTER-BASED SMOOTHING

In Liu and Croft [107], documents are clustered using a cosine similarity measure, and each document is smoothed with the cluster containing the document by interpolating the original maximum likelihood estimate $p_{ml}(w|\theta_D)$ with a cluster language model $p(w|Cluster)$, which is further smoothed by interpolating itself with a collection language model $p(w|C)$. That is:

$$
\begin{aligned}
p(w|\theta_D) &= \lambda p_{ml}(w|\theta_D) + (1-\lambda)p(w|Cluster) \\
&= \lambda p_{ml}(w|\theta_D) + (1-\lambda)[\beta p_{ml}(w|Cluster) + (1-\beta)p(w|C)],
\end{aligned}
$$

where $\lambda \in [0, 1]$ and $\beta \in [0, 1]$ are two parameters to be empirically set.

Intuitively, such a cluster-based smoothing method should be better than smoothing with the collection language model, which is also confirmed in [107], but the improvement is mostly insignificant. One possible reason may be because the two roles of smoothing have been mixed. Specifically, if the parameters are not set appropriately, the smoothing using cluster-based language model may actually end up penalizing terms common in the cluster due to the IDF effect of smoothing, thus lowering the scores of documents matching terms in the cluster (see Section 3.4). Indeed, if β is set to a very high value, $p_{ml}(w|Cluster)$ would be playing the role of a background model for smoothing.

A soft clustering strategy has been adopted to smooth document language models through using the Latent Dirichlet Allocation (LDA) model for clustering [118]. With this model, we assume that there exist k topics in the collection, each being characterized by a unigram language model θ_i. We can then replace $p(w|Cluster)$ with the following mixture of topic models:

$$p_{LDA}(w|Cluster) = \sum_{i=1}^{k} p(w|\theta_i)p(\theta_i|D) .$$

The probabilities $p(w|\theta_i)$ and $p(\theta_i|D)$ are obtained through fitting the LDA model to the collection [118]. In effect, this allows a document to be in multiple topics with some probabilities. Thus, smoothing of a document can involve an interpolation of potentially many topic clusters; this is different from [107] where just one cluster is used for smoothing. Results reported in [118] are encouraging. The LDA smoothing method outperforms the "hard clustering" method proposed in [107] consistently, but the experiments are all performed on relatively small collections, presumably due to the complexity of estimating the LDA model. The LDA model will be further discussed in Section 7.2.

4.1.2   DOCUMENT EXPANSION

A problem with smoothing a document using a cluster is that the cluster is not necessarily a good representation of similar documents to *every* document to be smoothed in the cluster. This is clearly the case when the document is at the boundary of the cluster (e.g., document d shown in Figure 4.1(a)). In such a case, the documents in the cluster would be a biased sample of the neighbors of the document to be smoothed as shown in Figure 4.1(a).

To address this problem, several researchers have proposed to construct a document-specific "neighborhood" in the document space, essentially to form a cluster for *every* document with the document at the center of the cluster. Intuitively, such a neighborhood contains the documents that are most similar to the document, thus serves well for smoothing. This is illustrated in Figure 4.1(b).

In [106], such document-centric clusters are constructed to obtain a representation of the corpus structure, and those clusters that are close to the query are then used to represent a document probabilistically in a low-dimension "corpus structure space." Documents are then scored using their corpus structure representation to compute the likelihood of the query. In effect, this achieves the goal of smoothing a document with the word distributions of the clusters covering the document. However, a major difference between this kind of smoothing based on dimension reduction and the interpolation-based smoothing we have discussed earlier is that it is difficult to control the amount of smoothing so that the original words in the document would have higher probabilities than the

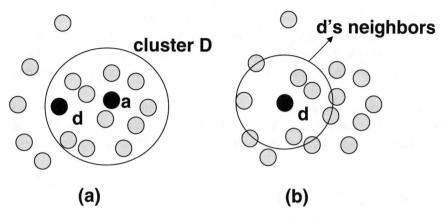

Figure 4.1: Cluster-based smoothing vs. document expansion (picture from [2]).

new words introduced through smoothing. As will be further discussed in Section 4.5, this scoring method can also be regarded as a case of a translation model.

In [2], such document-centric clusters are directly used for smoothing document language models. To improve the robustness of this smoothing method, the authors assign weights to the neighbors based on a cosine similarity measure so that a document farther away would contribute less to smoothing. They then use the probabilistic neighborhood to smooth the *count* of a word by interpolating the original count in the document with a weighted sum of counts of the word in the neighbor documents to obtain a smoothed count for each word. Such smoothed counts thus represent an "expanded document," and are then used as if they were the true counts of the words in the document for further smoothing with a collection language model. The count of word w in the new "expanded" document D' is given by:

$$c(w, D') = \alpha c(w, D) + (1 - \alpha) \sum_{X \in C-\{D\}} \left(\frac{sim(D, X)}{\sum_{Y \in C} sim(D, Y)} c(w, X) \right),$$

where $sim(D, X)$ is a similarity function (which is defined as the cosine measure in [2]).

Since the expanded counts are mainly affected by those neighbors with a high similarity to the current document D, in practice, we can use the closest neighbors for expansion to improve the efficiency. Note that such expansion can be done independently of any query, thus it can be done in the indexing stage.

Experiment results in [2] show that such a document expansion method not only outperforms the baseline simple smoothing method (i.e., with only a collection language model), but also outperforms the cluster-based smoothing method proposed in [107]. Moreover, it can be combined with pseudo feedback to further improve performance [2].

In [108], this neighborhood-based document expansion method is further extended to allow for smoothing with *remotely* related documents through probabilistic propagation of term counts.

This new smoothing method is shown to outperform the simple smoothing methods using a col-lection language model. It also achieves consistently better precision in the top-ranked documents than both cluster-based and document expansion smoothing methods. But interestingly, it has a worse mean average precision than the latter, indicating room for further research to improve this smoothing method.

The general idea of document expansion appears to be first explored in the vector space model for spoken document retrieval [119]. In [120], it has also been applied to topic detection and tracking through a probabilistic expansion based on the relevance model which we will introduce in Section 5.3.3.

4.2   BEYOND UNIGRAM MODELS

A natural extension of the basic query likelihood method is to go beyond unigram language models where the occurrence of words is assumed to be completely independent (an assumption obviously not holding) to capture some dependency between words. In this direction, Song and Croft [97] have studied using bigram and trigram language models. In a bigram language model, the generation of a current word would be dependent on the previous word generated, thus it can potentially capture adjacent words that can form phrases. Specifically, the query likelihood would be

$$p(Q|\theta_D) = p(q_1|\theta_D) \prod_{i=2}^{m} p(q_i|q_{i-1}, \theta_D)$$

where $p(q_i|q_{i-1}, \theta_D)$ is the conditional probability of generating query term q_i after we have just generated q_{i-1}.

While such n-gram models capture dependency based on word positions, other work has attempted to capture dependency based on grammar structures [121, 122, 123]. In all these ap-proaches, the retrieval formula eventually boils down to some combination of scores from matching units larger than single words (e.g., bigrams, head-modifier pairs, or collocation pairs) with scores from matching single words.

For example, in [123], the log-likelihood of a query given a document is defined as

$$\log p(Q|\theta_D) = \log p(L|D) + \sum_{i=1}^{m} \log p(q_i|D) + \sum_{(i,j)\in L} MI(q_i, q_j|L, D), \qquad (4.1)$$

where L is a pair-wise term linkage structure of the query Q obtained through parsing, and MI is the pointwise mutual information function. We can see that if the link structure L is empty, the last term in the equation would disappear, and we would thus recover the unigram query likelihood retrieval function. With a nonempty L, the last term captures term dependency.

Although these approaches have mostly shown benefit of capturing dependencies, the im-provement tends to be insignificant or at least not so significant as some other extensions that can achieve pseudo feedback effect. (These other extensions will be reviewed in the next chapter.) The general observation on these models is consistent with what researchers have observed on applying natural language processing techniques to improve indexing in traditional retrieval models, notably phrase-based indexing [39, 124, 40, 42].

One reason for these nonexciting results may be because as we move to more complex models to capture dependency, our data becomes even more sparse, making it difficult to obtain an accurate estimate of the model. Another more interesting explanation given in [92] is that the extra benefit of capturing dependency on top of a representation with independent single terms may not be as large as it appears to be. Specifically, it is shown in [92] that for ranking documents with a probabilistic model, a model assuming term independence is actually equivalent to any model assuming first-order dependency under a very weak assumption (called *proportional interdependence*). Intuitively, if a document already matches two words in a phrase, the document would already have a higher score than matching just one of them. Thus, the extra evidence from matching them as a phrase or in a particular order may not add that much on top of scoring based on single words.

A more successful retrieval model that can capture limited dependencies is the Markov Random Field model proposed in [54]. This model is a general discriminative model where arbitrary features can be combined in a retrieval function. In most of the applications of such a model, the features typically correspond to the scores of a document w.r.t. a query using an existing retrieval function such as the query likelihood, thus the Markov Random Field model essentially serves as a way to combine multiple scoring strategies, or to score with multiple representations. In particular, it has been shown that one can combine unigram language modeling scoring with bigram scoring as well as scoring based on word collocations within a small window of text to achieve better retrieval accuracy than using only unigram scoring [54].

4.3   PARSIMONIOUS LANGUAGE MODELS

All the methods for estimating document language models discussed so far rely on some kind of interpolation of word counts from some documents (e.g., the original document, similar documents, or all the documents in the collection). Thus, we can expect the estimated language model to give high probabilities to the common words which often do not carry much content. However, when a user poses a query, the user presumably would more likely use more discriminative, content-carrying words. Thus, if we are to use the document language model to model the queries (as it should based on the discussion in Section 3.1), intuitively we would also like the document language model to be more discriminative and assign high probabilities to content-carrying words rather than common words in English.

To realize this intuition, it was proposed in [89] that a two-component mixture model (called "distillation mixture model") can be used to estimate a more discriminative query model and document model. The basic idea is to assume that there exists some "noise" in a query or document which would be modeled with the collection background language model, and further assume that a query or a document is generated by sampling words from a mixture of the background model and a topic model to be estimated. When fitting such a model to a query or a document by forcing the use of the background model, the estimated topic model would be more discriminative. It was shown in [89] that applying such a distillation model to queries can improve performance. A similar model can be used for pseudo feedback, which will be further discussed in detail in Section 5.3.1.

The distillation idea was further generalized by Hiemstra and co-authors [125] to formulate *parsimonious* language models uniformly for queries, documents, and feedback. However, such parsimonious models have not shown significant improvement in retrieval accuracy, although they can be useful for reducing the index size [125]. Given the complicated interactions of smoothing and TF-IDF weighting, the insignificant improvement of performance may be caused by nonoptimal smoothing. Thus, further exploration may be needed to draw definitive conclusions about such parsimonious models.

4.4   FULL BAYESIAN QUERY LIKELIHOOD

In all the work we have discussed so far, we estimate θ_D using a point estimator, which means we take our best guess of what θ_D is. Intuitively, there are uncertainties associated with our estimate, and our estimate may not be accurate. A potentially better method is thus to consider this uncertainty and use the posterior distribution of θ_D (i.e., $p(\theta_D|D)$) to compute the query likelihood.

Such a full Bayesian treatment was proposed and studied in Zaragoza et al. [126]. The new scoring function is:

$$p(Q|D) = \int_{\Theta_D} p(Q|\theta_D)p(\theta_D|D)d\theta_D \,,$$

where Θ_D is the space of all possible multinomial distributions.

The regular query likelihood scoring formula can be seen as a special case of this more general query likelihood when we assume that $p(\theta_D|D)$ is entirely concentrated at one single point.

Although the integral looks intimidating, it actually has a closed form solution when we use a conjugate prior for computing the posterior distribution $p(\theta_D|D)$. The final ranking formula based on log-likelihood of a query given a document is [126]:

$$\log p(Q|D) \overset{\text{rank}}{=} \sum_{w \in Q \cap D} \sum_{i=1}^{c(w,Q)} \log(1 + \frac{c(w,D)}{\alpha_w + i - 1}) - \sum_{j=1}^{|Q|} \log(|D| + n_\alpha + j - 1) \qquad (4.2)$$

where α_w is a hyperparameter which can be set to $n_\alpha p(w|C)$, n_α will be empirically set, similar to the smoothing parameter μ in the Dirichlet prior smoothing method (see Section 3.3). Clearly, $n_\alpha = \sum_{w \in V} \alpha_w$.

This scoring formula is not much more expensive than a scoring formula using simple smoothing, thus this full Bayesian query likelihood retrieval function can be potentially used in a large-scale retrieval application system. Unfortunately, empirical evaluation shows that this new model, while theoretically very interesting, does not outperform the simple query likelihood function significantly. However, when this new model is combined with linear interpolation smoothing, the performance is better than any other combinations of existing smoothing methods. This may suggest that the new model cannot model the query noise very well, thus it can be substantially improved when combined with the linear interpolation to obtain the extra smoothing needed for modeling query noise. As the authors pointed out, it would be interesting to further study how to model the query noise using a full Bayesian model.

4.5   TRANSLATION MODEL

The work mentioned so far is all based on the same query likelihood scoring function which essentially performs the retrieval task through *exact* keyword matching in a way similar to a traditional retrieval model. In order to allow *inexact* matching of semantically related words and address the issues of synonym and polysemy, Berger and Lafferty proposed a very important extension to the basic exact matching query likelihood function by allowing the query likelihood to be computed based on a *translation model* of the form $p(u|v)$, which gives the probability that word v can be "semantically translated" to word u [110].

Formally, in this new model, the query likelihood is computed in the following way for a query $Q = q_1...q_m$:

$$p(Q|D) = \prod_{i=1}^{m} \sum_{w \in V} p(q_i|w)p(w|\theta_D) ,$$

where $p(q_i|w)$ is the probability of "translating" word w into q_i. This translation model can be understood intuitively by imagining a user who likes document D would formulate a query in two steps. In the first, the user would sample a word using the document model θ_D; in the second, the user would "translate" the word into another possibly different, but semantically related word to use as a query term.

We may also regard such a translation model as performing "semantic smoothing" in the sense that the translation model is equivalent to smoothing a document language model in the following way for the query likelihood retrieval function:

$$p(w|\theta_D) = \sum_{w' \in V} p(w|w')p(w'|D) .$$

It is easy to see that if $p(q_i|w)$ only allows a word to be translated into itself, we would recover the simple exact matching query likelihood. In general, of course, $p(q_i|w)$ would allow us to translate w into other semantically related words by giving them a nonzero translation probability. This enables us to score a document by counting the matches between a query word and a different but semantically related word in the document. A major challenge here is to estimate the translation model $p(q_i|w)$.

Translation models have originally been proposed for performing statistical machine translation by IBM researchers [16]. There are many variants of translation models with different levels of complexity (often called IBM translation models). The translation model $p(q_i|w)$ is the most primitive translation model [110]. In order to estimate this model, we will need some relevant query-document pairs where we know that the document is relevant to the query (i.e., relevance judgments).

Unfortunately, we generally do not have such training data available because it is labor-intensive to obtain many relevance judgments.

As an approximation, Berger and Lafferty used a heuristic method to generate some synthetic query-document pairs for training the translation model. Using this method, they have shown that the translation model can improve retrieval performance significantly over the baseline exact matching query likelihood [110].

An alternative way of estimating the translation model based on document titles was proposed in [127], which has also been shown to be effective. Furthermore, WordNet and co-occurrences of words have been exploited to define the translation model $p(q_i|w)$ in [128], and improvement of performance is observed. Clearly, the clickthroughs collected by a Web search engine can also serve as training data for estimating the translation model.

Another challenge in using such a model in a practical system is how to improve the scoring efficiency as we now have to consider many other words for possible matching for each query word. Indeed, evaluation of this method in TREC-8 has revealed that there are significant challenges in handling the large number of parameters and scoring all the documents efficiently [129]. As a result, in [129], a working set of documents are first selected using some heuristics such as filtering out any document that does not match at least one query word, and then each document in the working set is scored sequentially. However, such a strategy does not fully take advantage of the capacity of the translation model to potentially retrieve relevant documents that do not match any query word.

Despite these challenges, theoretically, the translation model provides a principled way to support semantic matching of related words, thus it is an important contribution in extending the basic query likelihood retrieval model. Such a model has also later been used successfully in applying language models to cross-lingual information retrieval [130].

The cluster-based query likelihood method proposed in [106] can be regarded as a form of a translation model where the whole document is "translated" into a query as a single unit through a set of clusters, giving the following query likelihood formula:

$$p(Q|D) = \sum_{G_i \in G} p(Q|G_i)p(G_i|D) ,$$

where G_i is a cluster of documents and G is a pre-constructed set of clusters of documents in the collection. This method has shown some improvement over the simple query likelihood method when combined with the simple query likelihood method, but does not perform well alone. Since the translation of a document into a cluster G_i causes loss of information, matching based on the clusters may not be discriminative enough to distinguish relevant documents from nonrelevant ones even though it can potentially increase recall due to the allowed inexact matching of terms. This may explain why the method alone does not perform well, but would perform much better when combined with a basic model that can supply the needed word-level discrimination. Similar observations have also been made in [32].

4.6   SUMMARY

In this chapter, we reviewed a number of models that all attempted to extend the basic query likeli-hood retrieval method in various ways and that are all substantially more expensive to compute than the basic model. Many of the extensions have not really led to significant improvement over the basic model. Given their complexity and the relative insignificant improvement (compared with models to be reviewed in the next chapter), most of these models have not found widespread applications except for the translation model which has been applied to cross-lingual IR tasks successfully. However, document-specific smoothing, especially document expansion, has been shown to improve retrieval accuracy significantly over those simple smoothing methods. Although they are also computationally expensive, the computation can be done in advance in the stage of indexing, so using such methods in a large-scale application system is still feasible.

Parsimonious models and full Bayesian query likelihood are quite interesting from theoretical perspective, and may have potential for more significant improvement of performance even though the current studies have only shown insignificant improvement.

CHAPTER 5

Probabilistic Distance Retrieval Model

In the previous two chapters, we have discussed simple and complex query likelihood retrieval models. All these models are based on the query likelihood scoring strategy, in which documents are ranked based on the likelihood of a query given a document. A major deficiency of the query likelihood retrieval models is that it cannot easily incorporate relevance or pseudo-relevance feedback. In this chapter, we introduce a new family of models called probabilistic distance retrieval models that can better accommodate feedback.

In these models, we would represent a document with a document language model and represent a query with a query language model. We then score a document with respect to a query based on the distance (or equivalently similarity) between the corresponding document language model and the query language model as measured using some probabilistic distance measure such as Kullback-Leibler (KL) divergence or cross entropy. Feedback can be naturally cast as to improve the estimate of the query language model based on the feedback information. These models are essentially similar to the traditional vector-space model except that text representation is based on probability distributions rather than heuristically weighted term vectors. This difference gives these probabilistic distance models an advantage over the vector-space model in optimizing term weighting because with a probabilistic text representation, we can leverage statistical estimation methods to optimize text representation. Also, the popular choice of the KL-divergence (and equivalently cross entropy) measure as the distance function can actually be shown to cover the query likelihood retrieval model as a special case when the query model is estimated based on only the query. Thus, these models can also be regarded as a generalization of the query likelihood retrieval model to better accommodate feedback.

5.1 DIFFICULTY IN SUPPORTING FEEDBACK WITH QUERY LIKELIHOOD

Feedback is an important technique to improve retrieval accuracy (see Section 1.1). Both relevance feedback and pseudo feedback have been well supported in traditional models (e.g., Rocchio [34] for the vector space model and term reweighting for the classical probabilistic model Feedback [56]). Naturally, in the early days when the query likelihood scoring method was introduced, people also explored feedback [131, 76, 132].

However, unlike in the traditional models where feedback can be naturally accommodated, in the query likelihood retrieval method, it is rather awkward to support feedback. The problem is caused by the fact that in all the query likelihood retrieval methods, the query is regarded as a sample of some kind of language model. Thus, it would not make much sense to talk about improving the query by adding additional terms and/or adjusting weights of those terms as done in the vector space model [34] because the new query created in this way would conceptually no longer be a sample of a language model.

It is also difficult to leverage feedback information to improve the estimate of a component model in the query likelihood retrieval model. Specifically, in the query likelihood retrieval model, we are most interested in improving our estimate of the document language model θ_D, but unfortunately we cannot use a user's feedback documents to improve our estimate of θ_D for any *unseen* document D. Indeed, θ_D is meant to be a model for the queries posed by users when they want to retrieve document D, thus the natural sample for θ_D would have to be a set of queries from users who think document D is relevant. This is in contrast with a classical probabilistic model such as the Binary Independence Retrieval Model [56], where feedback documents can be naturally used to improve our estimate of a component model (e.g., the relevant document model $p(D|Q, R = r)$) (see Section 2.2)).

Thus, with the query likelihood retrieval model, we do not have a principled natural way to improve the retrieval performance for the *current* query based on the feedback documents collected for the query.

Due to this difficulty, early work on achieving feedback using the query likelihood scoring method tends to be quite heuristic, and the techniques used are often not as elegant as the query likelihood method itself. For example, in [131], terms with high probabilities in the feedback documents but low probabilities in the collection are selected using a ratio approach as additional query terms. The method generally performs well, similar to Rocchio [34]. However, this ratio approach is conceptually restricted to the view of query as a set of terms, so it can not be applied to the more general case when the query is considered as a sequence of terms in order to incorporate the frequency information of a query term. Also, the influence of feedback cannot be controlled through term weighting; a term is either added to the query or not.

Miller and others [76] take feedback essentially as expanding the original query with all terms in the feedback documents. Terms are pooled into bins by the number of feedback documents in which they occur, and for each bin, a different transition probability in the HMM is heuristically estimated[1]. The performance of such a feedback technique is quite promising and robust. However, the interpretation of a query both as a text (generated by an HMM) and as a set of terms is conceptually inconsistent. It also involves heuristic adjustment of transition probabilities by incorporating document frequency to "filter" out the high frequency words.

In [132], two interesting ideas about feedback have been explored. First, a feedback criterion based on the optimization of the scores of feedback documents is developed, which turns out to be actually very similar to the ratio approach used in [131]. Second, a threshold for the number

---

[1] As a result, the smoothing is no longer equivalent to the simple linear interpolation as is in their basic HMM.

of selected terms is heuristically derived from the score optimization criterion. This approach is reported to be effective [132], but again it still causes inconsistency in interpreting the query.

Several studies [132, 100, 133, 109] have used feedback documents to optimize the smoothing parameter or query term reweighting. While these methods do not cause conceptual inconsistency, they also do not achieve full benefit of feedback due to the limited use of feedback information.

Interestingly, with the query likelihood retrieval model, we can naturally use the judged relevant documents from the *current* user to improve search accuracy for those *future* users who may be interested in retrieving any of these relevant documents. Specifically, a search engine system can collect all the feedback information (e.g., queries and associated relevant documents) from the users, group all the queries associated with each (relevant) document D, and use these queries to improve our estimate of θ_D, thus helping future users who are interested in retrieving any of these documents. Actually, even without explicitly judged feedback information, a search engine can still leverage this strategy to perform massive implicit feedback. For example, a search engine can record the queries and associated clickthroughs from users; by assuming that a clicked (i.e., viewed) document is relevant, we can group all the queries associated with clicking on document D, and use them to improve the estimate of θ_D.

5.2 KULLBACK-LEIBLER DIVERGENCE RETRIEVAL MODEL

The difficulty in supporting feedback with query likelihood scoring has motivated the development of a probabilistic distance model called Kullback-Leibler (KL) divergence retrieval model [1, 134]. This KL-divergence retrieval model was first proposed in [1] within the risk minimization retrieval framework (see Section 2.5), which introduces the concept of query language model (in additional to the document language model) and models the retrieval problem as a statistical decision problem [1, 89, 90]. However, KL-divergence had previously been used for distributed information retrieval [135].

In this KL-divergence model, we define two different language models, one for a query (θ_Q) and one for a document (θ_D). That is, we will assume that the query is a sample observed from a query language model θ_Q, while the document a sample from a document language model θ_D. Intuitively, the query model θ_Q captures what the user is interested in, while θ_D captures the topic of document D. We can then use the KL-divergence of these two models to measure how close they are to each other and use their distance (indeed, negative distance) as a score to rank documents. This way, the closer the document model is to the query model, the higher the document would be ranked.

Formally, the score of a document D w.r.t. a query Q is given by:

$$Score(D, Q) = -D(\theta_Q || \theta_D)$$

$$= - \sum_{w \in V} p(w|\theta_Q) \log \frac{p(w|\theta_Q)}{p(w|\theta_D)}$$

$$= \sum_{w \in V} p(w|\theta_Q) \log p(w|\theta_D) - \sum_{w \in V} p(w|\theta_Q) \log p(w|\theta_Q) \ .$$

Since the last term is query entropy and does not affect ranking of documents, ranking based on negative KL-divergence is the same as ranking based on the negative cross entropy, $\sum_{w \in V} p(w|\theta_Q) \log p(w|\theta_D)$.

Note that although ranking based on KL-divergence and ranking based on cross entropy are equivalent in the ad hoc retrieval setting, where we always compare documents for the *same* query and can thus ignore any document-independent constant, they would generate quite different results when we compare scores across *different* queries as in the case of filtering or topic detection and tracking [43]. Specifically, one measure may generate scores more comparable across queries than the other, depending on whether including the query entropy makes sense. For a detailed analysis of this difference and an attempt to obtain a unified way of normalizing scores for both ad hoc retrieval and topic tracking, see [43].

With the KL-divergence retrieval model, the retrieval task is reduced to two subtasks, i.e., estimating θ_Q and θ_D respectively. The estimation of document model θ_D is similar to that in the query likelihood retrieval model, but the estimation of query model θ_Q offers interesting opportunities of leveraging feedback information to improve retrieval accuracy. Specifically, feedback information can be exploited to improve our estimate of θ_Q. Such a feedback method is called *model–based feedback* in [134].

On the surface, the KL-divergence model appears to be quite different from the query likelihood method. However, it turns out that it is easy to show that the KL-divergence model covers the query likelihood method as a special case when we use the empirical query word distribution to estimate θ_Q, i.e.,

$$p(w|\theta_Q) = \frac{c(w, Q)}{|Q|} \ .$$

Indeed, with such an estimate, we have :

$$score(D, Q) \overset{rank}{=} \sum_{w \in V} p(w|\theta_Q) \log p(w|\theta_D)$$

$$= \sum_{w \in V} \frac{c(w, Q)}{|Q|} \log p(w|\theta_D)$$

$$\overset{rank}{=} \sum_{w \in V} c(w, Q) \log p(w|\theta_D)$$

$$= \log p(Q|\theta_D) \ .$$

In this sense, the KL-divergence model is a generalization of the query likelihood scoring method with the additional advantage of supporting feedback more naturally.

Moreover, if we use the same general smoothing scheme discussed in Section 3.3 (i.e., smoothing a document language model θ_D with a collection language model), with similar transformations to those in Section 3.4, we can also show that the KL-divergence retrieval function can be rewritten as:

$$score(D, Q) \stackrel{\text{rank}}{=} \sum_{w \in D} p(w|\theta_Q) \log \frac{p_s(w|\theta_D)}{\alpha_D p(w|C)} + \log \alpha_D . \tag{5.1}$$

When $p(w|\theta_Q)$ is estimated using the empirical word distribution in the query, it would be zero for all the words except for the query words. This makes it efficient to score documents with the KL-divergence retrieval function. However, the main motivation for using this model (instead of the query likelihood retrieval model) is so that we can improve the estimate of θ_Q based on additional information such as feedback documents, and an improved estimate of θ_Q may give nonzero probabilities to potentially many other nonquery words. This clearly would cause a concern of scoring efficiency.

A common solution to this problem is that we truncate the query language model θ_Q so that we only keep the highest probability words according to $p(w|\theta_Q)$. Specifically, we can set the probabilities of low-probability words to zero, and possibly renormalize the probabilities of the remaining words. With a truncated query model, the KL-divergence retrieval model can be computed very efficiently with the help of an inverted index. Indeed, the sum would be over only those terms that both occur in document D and have nonzero probabilities according to the truncated query model θ_Q.

Thus, the generalization of query likelihood as KL-divergence would not incur much extra computational overhead; yet, it has the advantage of accommodating feedback through improving the estimate of the query language model based on feedback documents. The KL-divergence represents the state of the art of the language modeling approaches to retrieval. The best retrieval performance is often achieved through using the KL-divergence retrieval model with appropriate methods for estimating document language model θ_D (e.g., Dirichlet prior) and estimating query language model θ_Q (e.g., the mixture model [134] or relevance model [71]).

It is worth pointing out that although the scoring formula of the KL-divergence retrieval model can be regarded as a generalization of the formula for the query likelihood retrieval model, the document language model θ_D can be interpreted differently in the KL-divergence retrieval model than in the query likelihood retrieval model. Specifically, we may interpret θ_D in the KL-divergence retrieval model in two differently ways: (1) We can interpret θ_D in the same way as we do for the θ_D in the query likelihood retrieval model, i.e., take it as defining a model of the words expected to be used in a query to retrieve D. With this interpretation, we can interpret the KL-divergence score as measuring how close this model is to the estimated actual model used to generate the current query. (2) We can interpret θ_D as a "real" document model, i.e., the language model used to generate document D. With this second interpretation, the KL-divergence score would mean the distance between this document language model, which represents the content of the document, and the query language model, which represents the user's information need as described by the query.

Although the first interpretation is more consistent with the query likelihood retrieval model, it is the second interpretation that makes the KL-divergence more flexible to incorporate feedback and document expansion. Indeed, the second interpretation is completely in parallel to the vector-space model with the main difference being a probabilistic representation of text in the KL-divergence model vs. a heuristic vector representation of text in the vector-space model (see Section 2.1). The decoupling of the similarity/distance function from text representation offers the flexibility to improve the query language model and document language model independently. As a result, we can easily leverage all kinds of feedback information to improve the query language model, which intuitively improves our representation of the user's information need. Similarly, we can also improve our estimate of the document language model based on related documents or any additional information about the document (e.g., tags assigned through social tagging or anchor text in a hypertext collection). However, as in the case of the vector-space model, the decoupling also has a disadvantage—it makes it harder to interpret the scoring method from the viewpoint of capturing relevance. For example, there are other divergence-based measures (e.g., Jensen-Shannon divergence [136]), so one might wonder whether some other probabilistic distance measures might even perform better than the KL-divergence.

The KL-divergence model itself offers no answer to such a question. Fortunately, the first interpretation of θ_D discussed above provides some justification for the use of the KL-divergence (since the query likelihood retrieval model can be justified based on the probability ranking principle, see Section 2.2). To address this deficiency, we can use the axiomatic retrieval framework to analyze different distance functions to see whether they satisfy the constraints that capture effective retrieval heuristics. For example, in [137], several divergence functions are analyzed and the results show that the Jensen-Shannon divergence cannot satisfy an important length normalization constraint, and its empirical results are significantly worse than the KL-divergence.

5.3   ESTIMATION OF QUERY MODELS

With the KL-divergence retrieval model, feedback can be achieved through re-estimating the query model θ_Q based on feedback information. Several methods have been proposed to improve the estimate of the query model in the setting of pseudo feedback, i.e., improving the estimate of θ_Q by exploiting the top-ranked documents. Interestingly, the relevance feedback setting appears to have not attracted much attention, likely because in real applications, it is often unrealistic to obtain many examples of relevant documents. Technically, we can adapt these pseudo feedback methods to handle relevance feedback by replacing the top-ranked documents with real examples of relevant documents. However, as we will further discuss in Section 5.4, feedback based on only negative information (i.e., nonrelevant information) remains challenging even with the KL-divergence retrieval model [138]. We now discuss several different methods for estimating a query model based on feedback documents.

5.3.1 MODEL-BASED FEEDBACK

Zhai and Lafferty [134] proposed two methods for estimating an improved query model θ_Q using feedback documents. Both methods follow the basic idea of interpolating an existing query model (e.g., one estimated based on the empirical query word distribution) with an estimated feedback topic model.

Specifically, let θ_Q be the current query model and θ_F be a feedback topic model estimated based on (positive) feedback documents $F = \{D_1, ..., D_{|F|}\}$. The updated new query model θ'_Q is given by

$$p(w|\theta'_Q) = (1 - \alpha)p(w|\theta_Q) + \alpha p(w|\theta_F)$$

where $\alpha \in [0, 1]$ is a parameter to control the amount of feedback. When $\alpha = 0$, we end up with no query model updating, while setting $\alpha = 1$ would essentially ignore the original query and completely reset the query model to the one estimated based on feedback documents only.

How to set parameter α is a major technical challenge in this approach. Intuitively, for relevance feedback, α can be set to a relatively high value. However, for pseudo feedback, α should not be set to a high value as it has the risk of causing query concept drift; because the feedback documents may be biased, over-trusting θ_F needs to be prevented by retaining a sufficient amount of probability mass for the original query model θ_Q. However, if α is too small, we may not fully take advantage of feedback. Thus, how to optimize α is a very difficult question especially when no reliable relevance judgments are available as in the case of pseudo feedback. There has been some follow-up work to address this problem in pseudo feedback [139], which we will further discuss in Section 5.3.1.3. In practice, this parameter can always be set empirically using cross-validation (i.e., based on optimization on some training data).

We now introduce the two methods proposed in [134] for estimating θ_F with F.

5.3.1.1 Mixture Model Feedback

One approach uses a two-component mixture model to fit the feedback documents where one component is a fixed background language model $p(w|C)$ estimated using the collection and the other is an unknown, to-be-discovered topic model $p(w|\theta_F)$. Essentially, the words in F are assumed to fall into two kinds: (1) background words (to be explained by $p(w|C)$) and (2) topical words (to be explained by $p(w|\theta_F)$). By fitting such a mixture model to the data, we can "factor out" the background words and obtain a discriminative topic model which would assign high probabilities to words that are frequent in the feedback documents but not frequent in the collection (thus not well explained by $p(w|C)$).

Specifically, when we generate a word using this mixture model, we would first decide which model to use and then sample a word using the chosen model. Thus, the probability of generating a word w is:

$$p(w) = (1 - \lambda)p(w|\theta_F) + \lambda p(w|C)$$

where $\lambda \in [0, 1]$ is the probability of choosing the background model $p(.|C)$ to generate the word.

Thus the log-likelihood function for the entire set of feedback documents is:

$$\log p(F|\theta_F) = \sum_{w \in V} c(w, F) \log((1 - \lambda)p(w|\theta_F) + \lambda p(w|C))$$

where $c(w, F)$ is the count of word w in the set of feedback documents F.

Intuitively, λ indicates how much weight we want to put on the background model, and can be interpreted as the amount of background words we would like to factor out.

The topic model θ_F can be obtained by using the ML estimator. That is, we would tune θ_F to best fit the feedback documents. Intuitively, θ_F and the background model $p(.|C)$ would work together to explain the words in the feedback documents, thus if we want to maximize the likelihood function, θ_F should assign high probabilities to those words that have small probabilities according to $p(.|C)$ and assign small probabilities to those words with high probabilities according to $p(.|C)$ so that they can work together "efficiently" to maximize the likelihood function.

Note that in attempting to find the optimal θ_F using the ML estimator, we need to set λ to a fixed value. The reason is if we allow λ to change freely, the ML estimator would tend to set it to zero. This is because $p(w|C)$ is set to the collection language model, thus it cannot change, but $p(w|\theta_F)$ can freely change. Thus, to maximize the likelihood, it would be intuitively better not to use $p(w|C)$ unless it can perfectly explain the word frequencies in F (i.e., it is the ML estimate of a unigram language model for F), which is unlikely.

How should we set λ? Intuitively, if we set λ to a larger value, we would force the collection background model $p(w|C)$ to be used more often when generating a word in a feedback document, which is equivalent to saying that we believe that there is more noise in the feedback documents. In effect, this would "encourage" the estimated topic model θ_F to focus more on the words with small probabilities by $p(w|C)$ than on those with large probabilities. That is, θ_F would more likely assign high probabilities to discriminative words.

The ML estimate of θ_F can be computed using the Expectation-Maximization (EM) algorithm [140]. The EM algorithm is a hill-climbing algorithm. We would start with a random initialization of θ_F, and then repeatedly improve θ_F to increase the likelihood until the algorithm converges to a local maximum of the likelihood function. Specifically, the EM algorithm would improve θ_F by iteratively alternating between an E-step and an M-step.

In the E-step, we would use the following equation to compute the posterior probability of a word w being generated using θ_F (or $p(.|C)$) based on the current estimate of θ_F:

E-step: $p(z_w = 1) = \frac{(1-\lambda)p^{(n)}(w|\theta_F)}{(1-\lambda)p^{(n)}(w|\theta_F) + \lambda p(w|C)}$

where $z_w \in \{0, 1\}$ is a hidden variable indicating whether word w is generated using the topic model θ_F ($z_w = 1$) or the collection model $p(w|C)$ ($z_w = 0$).

Intuitively, we try to "guess" which model has been used to generate word w. If $p(w|\theta_F)$ is much larger than $p(w|C)$, then we would guess that w is more likely generated using θ_F, and $p(z_w = 1)$ would be high. The reason why we want to figure out which model has been used to generate w is so that we know which words in the feedback documents belong to θ_F and we would use them to improve our estimate of θ_F. Indeed, if we knew which words are generated using θ_F

(instead of $p(.|C)$), estimation of θ_F would be very easy since all we need to do is to get the count of every such word (i.e., $c(w, F)$ for a word known to be generated from θ_F) and normalize these counts to obtain the probability of each word $p(w|\theta_F)$. However, $p(z_w = 1)$ does not tell us for sure whether word w is generated using θ_F. Thus, in the M-step of the EM algorithm, we would use a discounted word count (i.e., $c(w, F)p(z_w = 1)$) for estimating $p(w|\theta_F)$. A word count is discounted more if $p(z_w = 1)$ is small, which makes sense because a small $p(z_w = 1)$ indicates that word w is unlikely generated using θ_F, thus word w should not contribute much to our estimate of θ_F.

Formally, in the M-step, we use the following equation to update our estimate of θ_F:

M-step: $p^{(n+1)}(w \mid \theta_F) = \frac{c(w,F)p(z_w=1)}{\sum_{w' \in V} c(w',F)p(z_{w'}=1)}$.

The EM algorithm is guaranteed to converge to a local maximum of the likelihood function [140]. In our case, given λ, the feedback documents $\mathcal{F}$, and the collection language model $p(w|C)$, the likelihood function has just one local maximum, so we are guaranteed to find the global maximum. A detailed derivation of this EM algorithm can be found in [141].

5.3.1.2 Divergence Minimization Feedback

The other approach proposed in [134] uses an idea similar to Rocchio in the vector space model [34] and assumes that θ_F is a language model that is very close to the language model of every document in the feedback document set F, but far away from the collection language model which can be regarded as an approximation of nonrelevant language model. The distance between language models is measured using KL-divergence.

Specifically, the problem of computing θ_F is cast as solving the following optimization problem:

$$\hat{\theta}_F = \arg\min_{\theta_F} \left([\frac{1}{|F|} \sum_{i=1}^{|F|} D(\theta_F||\theta_i)] - \lambda D(\theta_F||\theta_C) \right)$$

where θ_i is a smoothed language model estimated using document $D_i \in F$, θ_C is the background collection language model $p(w|C)$, and $\lambda \in [0, 1)$ is a parameter to control the distance between the estimated θ_F and the background model θ_C. When $\lambda = 0$, we ignore the background model and the estimated θ_F would be the average of language models for each document in F. As we increase λ, we would force θ_F to be different from the background model, thus it would tend to assign smaller probabilities to the common words in the collection and the model would be more discriminative.

Observing the constraint $\sum_{w \in V} p(w|\theta_F) = 1$, we can use the Lagrange Multiplier approach [11] to solve this optimization problem and obtain the following analytical solution:

$$p(w|\hat{\theta}_F) \propto \exp\left(\frac{1}{1-\lambda} \frac{1}{|F|} \sum_{i=1}^{|F|} \log p(w|\theta_i) - \frac{\lambda}{1-\lambda} \log p(w|C) \right) .$$

This solution is intuitively quite reasonable: the estimated feedback topic model $\hat{\theta}_F$ would assign a high probability to a word with high average frequency in the feedback documents but low frequency in the collection. Note that once again the collection language model θ_C has helped to achieve an IDF effect.

Both the mixture model method and the divergence minimization method are shown to be quite effective for pseudo feedback with performance comparable to or better than Rocchio [134]. However, both methods (especially divergence minimization) are also shown to be sensitive to parameter settings.

5.3.1.3   Robust Mixture Model

When using the mixture model discussed in Section 5.3.1.1 for pseudo feedback, we have to set several parameters empirically: (1) the interpolation parameter α; (2) the background model weight λ; and (3) the number of top-ranked documents to be used for feedback. Although we may set these parameters empirically (e.g., using cross validation), the optimal values of these parameters likely depend on the specific query and specific document collection. Thus, it would be desirable to somehow eliminate these parameters or improve the robustness of such a model to the setting of these parameters. Some follow-up work has indeed attempted to achieve this goal [142, 139].

In [142], the mixture model was extended to better integrate the original query model with the feedback documents and to allow each feedback document to potentially contribute differently to the estimated feedback topic language model. The extended model is shown to be relatively more robust than the original model, but the model is still quite sensitive to the number of documents used for pseudo feedback [142]. Moreover, due to the use of several priors, this new model has more prior parameters that need to be set manually with little guidance.

In Tao and Zhai [139], these prior parameters were eliminated through a regularized EM algorithm and a more robust pseudo feedback model is established. Indeed, it has been shown that with no parameter tuning, the model delivers comparable performance to a well-tuned baseline pseudo feedback model.

The main ideas introduced in this new model and estimation method are the following: (1) Each feedback document is allowed to have a potentially different amount of noisy words, and the amount of noise is automatically estimated with no need of manual tuning. This makes it more robust with respect to the number of documents used for pseudo feedback. (2) The interpolation of the original query model with the feedback model is implemented by treating the original query model as a prior in a Bayesian estimation framework. This makes the interpolation more meaningful and offers the opportunity to dynamically change the interpolation weights during the estimation process. (3) The parameter estimation process (EM algorithm) is carefully regularized so that we would start with the original query model and gradually enrich it with additional words picked up from the feedback documents. Such regularization ensures that the estimated model stays close to the original query. (4) This gradual enrichment process stops when "sufficient" new words have been picked up by the EM algorithm, where "sufficient" roughly corresponds to reaching a balance between the original query model and the new topic model picked up from the feedback documents (i.e., interpolation with a 0.5 weight).

Specifically, in this new model, each document D has its own mixing weight λ_D in the mixture model. Thus, the log-likelihood function is:

$$\log p(F|\theta_F) = \sum_{D \in F} \sum_{w \in V} c(w, D) \log((1 - \lambda_D) p(w|\theta_F) + \lambda_D p(w|C)) \,.$$

The query is combined with the feedback model through a conjugate (Dirichlet) prior on θ_F defined based on Q:

$$p(\theta_F) \propto \prod_{w \in V} p(w|\theta_F)^{\mu p(w|Q)} \,,$$

where μ is a parameter indicating the strength of the prior, and $p(w|Q)$ is the empirical query word distribution. In effect, such a prior forces the estimated θ_F to be as close to $p(w|Q)$ as possible; the larger μ is, the closer θ_F would be to $p(w|Q)$.

Using the Maximum A Posteriori (MAP) estimator and a noninformative (i.e., uniform) prior on λ_D's, we have

$$\hat{\theta}_F = \arg \max_{\theta} p(F|\theta_F) p(\theta_F) \,.$$

The MAP estimate can also be computed using the EM algorithm with a slightly modified M-step that incorporates the pseudo counts of words from the prior. The EM algorithm would also allow us to estimate the parameter λ_D simultaneously. This means that we have an additional equation for updating our estimate of λ_D in the M-step.

To solve the problem of setting μ, a regularized EM algorithm is used. The idea is to start with a very high value for μ and then gradually reduce μ. In effect, this is to make θ_F essentially the same as the prior (i.e., $p(w|Q)$) at the beginning, and then gradually allow it to be updated with topical word counts from the feedback documents. Since μ is being decreased, the prior pseudo counts would also be gradually decreased. At the same time, as we improve our estimate of the topic model, the new counts picked up from the feedback documents would gradually increase. Eventually, the pseudo counts from the prior and the new counts from the feedback documents would be roughly the same, at which point, the algorithm would be stopped.

With this robust mixture model and estimation method, we see that there is no parameter to set except for the number of documents to be used for pseudo feedback. Experiment results show that the model is more robust w.r.t. the choice of the number of documents for feedback than the original mixture model and can achieve near optimal performance without much parameter tuning [139].

A different approach to improving robustness of pseudo feedback is presented in Collins-Thompson and Callan [143], where the idea is to perform sampling over both the feedback documents and the query to generate alternative sets of feedback documents and alternative query variants. Feedback models obtained from each alternative set can then be combined to improve the robustness of the estimated feedback model. Experiments using a variant of the relevance model [71] as the baseline feedback method show that the proposed sampling method can improve the robustness of feedback even though not necessarily the retrieval accuracy of feedback.

5.3.2   MARKOV CHAIN QUERY MODEL ESTIMATION

Another approach to estimating a query model is to iteratively mine the entire corpus by following a Markov chain formed by documents and terms [1]. The basic idea of this approach is to exploit term co-occurrences to learn a translation model $p(u|v)$ to capture the semantic relations between words. Specifically, we hope that $p(u|v)$ would give a high probability to word u if it is semantically related to word v. With this translation model, we can then enrich the original query model estimated solely based on the query with potentially more related terms with nonzero probabilities.

Specifically, we can imagine a surfer iteratively following a Markov chain of the form $w_0 \rightarrow D_0 \rightarrow w_1 \rightarrow D_1...$ where w_i is a word and D_i a document, and the transition probability from a document D to a word w is given by the ML estimate of the document language model $p(w|D) = \frac{c(w,D)}{|D|}$, while the transition probability from word w to document D' is assumed to be the posterior probability:

$$p(D'|w) \propto p(w|D')p(D')$$

where $p(D')$ is a prior distribution over documents, and can be set based on additional information about a document such as its PageRank score [144], or simply set to uniform in the case of no additional information.

When visiting a word, the surfer is further assumed to stop at the word with probability $1 - \alpha$ which is a parameter to be empirically set. The translation probability $p(u|v)$ can then be defined as the probability of stopping at word u if the surfer starts with word v. Clearly, the same Markov chain can also be exploited to compute other translation probabilities such as $p(D'|D)$ ("translating" document D into document D') or $p(D|w)$ ("translating" word w into document D) without much modification.

Such a translation model intuitively would capture words that directly or indirectly co-occur with each other. The relative emphasis on direct occurrence vs. indirect co-occurrence is controlled by the parameter α. A larger α would encourage the surfer to explore more, and thus we would consider more indirect co-occurrences of words. In the extreme case of setting $\alpha = 0$, we would essentially only consider direct co-occurrences when computing the translation model. With the obtained translation model, we can now see how we can use it to estimate our query language model.

Suppose a user has an information need characterized by a query model θ_Q. We would assume that the user has formulated the current query $Q = q_1...q_m$ through sampling a word from θ_Q and then "translating" it to a query word in Q according to the translation model. Given the observed Q, we can then compute the posterior probability of a word being selected from θ_Q (to generate any query word in Q) and use this probability to estimate θ_Q:

$$p(w|\theta_Q) \propto \sum_{i=1}^{m} p(q_i|w)p(w|U)$$

where $p(w|U)$ is our prior probability of a word w would have been chosen by user U (which can be set to the collection language model $p(w|C)$ with no additional knowledge). We may also use this prior probability to filter out those "stop words" (i.e., noninformative common words in English) by setting their probabilities to zero.

Intuitively, this model exploits global co-occurrences of words to expand a query and obtain an enriched query language model. However, while such a global expansion has been shown to be effective, the expansion is much more effective if the Markov chain is restricted to going through the top-ranked documents for a query [1]. Thus, the method can also be regarded as a way to perform pseudo feedback with language models. The observation that local co-occurrence analysis is more effective than global co-occurrence analysis is also reported in a study of traditional retrieval model [145]. Intuitively, this is because the local documents (i.e., documents close to the query) can prevent noisy words being picked due to distracting co-occurrences in nonrelevant documents. Leveraging the top-ranked documents for co-occurrence analysis and query expansion (i.e., pseudo feedback) is an important general heuristic in information retrieval that often works well.

In Collins-Thompson and Callan [146], such a Markov chain expansion method has been extended to include multiple types of term associations, such as co-occurrences in an external corpus, co-occurrences in top-ranked search results, and term associations obtained from an external resource (e.g., WordNet). While the expansion accuracy is not better than a strong baseline expansion method, such a massive expansion strategy is shown to be more robust.

5.3.3   RELEVANCE MODEL

Yet another way to estimate the query language model is the *relevance model* developed by Lavrenko and Croft in [71]. While the motivation for this model comes from the difficulty in estimating model parameters in the classical probabilistic model when we do not have relevance judgments, the derived model also takes advantage of the top-ranked documents in the results from an initial round of retrieval to obtain a word distribution that can characterize the content of a relevant document. This is similar to a query model that characterizes what a user is interested in finding. And indeed, such a relevance model can be used as a query language model directly in the KL-divergence retrieval model.

Since the relevance model is motivated with the classical probabilistic model, we first take a look at the derivation of this model using the document-generation decomposition of the joint probability $p(Q, D|R)$ (see Section 2.2):

$$O(R|Q, D) \quad \propto \quad \frac{p(D|Q, R = r)}{p(D|Q, R = \bar{r})} \, .$$

We see that our main tasks are to estimate two document models, one for relevant documents (i.e., $p(D|Q, R = r)$) and one for nonrelevant documents (i.e., $p(D|Q, R = \bar{r})$). If we assume a multiple Bernoulli model for $p(D|Q, R)$, we will obtain precisely the Binary Independence Model pioneered by Robertson and Sparck Jones [56] and further studied by others (e.g., [61, 68]). The model parameters can be estimated by using some examples of relevant and nonrelevant documents, making this an attractive model for relevance feedback.

It was not immediately clear, though, how we can estimate the parameters *without* relevance judgments. Croft and Harper [68] studied this problem and introduced two approximations: (1) the nonrelevant document model $p(D|Q, R = \bar{r})$ can be estimated by assuming all the documents in the collection to be nonrelevant. (2) The relevant document model $p(D|Q, R = r)$ is assumed to give a constant probability to all the query words. Using these assumptions, they showed that this classical probabilistic model would lead to a scoring formula with IDF weighting for matched terms. This is indeed a very interesting derivation and provides some probabilistic justification of IDF. However, while the first assumption is reasonable, the second is clearly an over-simplification. A more reasonable approximation may be to use some top-ranked documents as an approximation of relevant documents, i.e., follow the idea of pseudo relevance feedback. This is essentially the idea behind the relevance model work [71].

In the relevance model, a multinomial model is used to model a document, thus we can capture the term frequency naturally. (Previously, 2-Poisson mixture models had been proposed as a member of the classical probabilistic models to model term frequency, and an approximation of that model has led to the effective BM25 retrieval function [70].) Using multinomial distribution, we have:

$$O(R|Q, D) \quad \propto \quad \frac{\prod_{i=1}^{n} p(d_i|Q, R = r)}{\prod_{i=1}^{n} p(d_i|Q, R = \bar{r})} \tag{5.2}$$

where document $D = d_1...d_n$.

Since $p(d_i|Q, R = \bar{r})$ can be reasonably approximated by $p(d_i|C)$ (i.e., collection language model), the main challenge is to estimate $p(d_i|Q, R = r)$, which captures word occurrences in relevant documents and is called a *relevance model*. In [71], the authors proposed two methods for estimating such a relevance model, both based on the idea of using the top-ranked documents to approximate relevant documents to estimate the relevance model $p(w|Q, R = r)$. Thus, this is essentially another way to leverage pseudo-relevance feedback, and the estimated relevance model $p(w|Q, R = r)$ can also be regarded as a query language model in the KL-divergence retrieval model. Indeed, although $p(w|Q, R = r)$ is meant to be a model for words in relevant documents, it intuitively represents what a user is interested in, which is precisely what a query language model attempts to capture. Moreover, in some later studies [92], it was shown that using the relevance model as a query model to score documents with the KL-divergence function works better than using it as a component in the classical probabilistic model for retrieval. This is why we have included the discussion of relevance model as a variant method for estimating query language models.

We now describe the two methods proposed in [71] for estimating the relevance model. In the first method (i.e., Model 1), the authors essentially use the query likelihood $p(Q|D)$ as a weight for document D and take an average of the probability of word w given by each document language model. Clearly, only the top ranked documents matter because other documents would have very small or zero weight. Formally, let Θ represent the set of smoothed document models in the collection and $Q = q_1...q_m$ be a query. The formula is derived as follows:[2]

$$
\begin{aligned}
p(w|Q, R = r) &= \sum_{\theta_D \in \Theta} p(w|\theta_D)p(\theta_D|Q, R = r) \\
&= \sum_{\theta_D \in \Theta} p(w|\theta_D)\frac{p(Q|\theta_D, R = r)p(\theta_D|R = r)}{p(Q|R = r)} \\
&\propto \sum_{\theta_D \in \Theta} p(w|\theta_D)p(Q|\theta_D, R = r)p(\theta_D|R = r) \\
&= \sum_{\theta_D \in \Theta} p(w|\theta_D)p(\theta_D|R = r)\prod_{i=1}^{m} p(q_i|\theta_D, R = r) .
\end{aligned}
$$

This estimate can be seen as a weighted average of $p(w|\theta_D)$ over all the documents in the collection. The weight for document D is $p(\theta_D|R = r)\prod_{i=1}^{m} p(q_i|\theta_D, R = r)$, in which the second term is precisely the query likelihood given the document, which tells us how likely the document is relevant to the query, while the first is a general prior on documents to favor a document that is more likely relevant to any query. Thus, the count of a word in a highly scored document according to the query likelihood retrieval model (more likely a relevant document) would be weighted more when combining the counts, which intuitively makes sense. $p(\theta_D|R = r)$ can be set based on additional information about a document such as the number of times it has been viewed or its PageRank score. In [71], it was set to uniform.

In the second method (i.e., Model 2), they compute the association between each word and the query using documents containing both query terms and the word as "bridges." The strongly associated words are then assigned high probabilities in the relevance model. Formally, the derivation is as follows:

$$
\begin{aligned}
p(w|Q, R = r) &= \frac{p(Q|w, R = r)p(w|R = r)}{p(Q|R = r)} \\
&\propto p(Q|w, R = r)p(w|R = r) \\
&= p(w|R = r)\prod_{i=1}^{m} p(q_i|w, R = r) \\
&= p(w|R = r)\prod_{i=1}^{m} \sum_{\theta_D \in \Theta} p(q_i|\theta_D, R = r)p(\theta_D|w, R = r) .
\end{aligned}
$$

Again, we added the relevance variable R to be consistent with our overall formal framework. Interestingly, adding this relevance variable also helps clarify the meaning of the term $p(w)$ in the original derivation in [71], which is now $p(w|R = r)$. Specifically, interpreting $p(w)$ as $p(w|R = r)$ means that it should favor words that tend to occur in any relevant document to any query. In [71],

---

[2]The derivation in the original paper does not contain the relevance variable R. We added it to be consistent with our overall formal framework for probabilistic retrieval.

it is estimated as

$$p(w|R = r) = \sum_{\theta_D \in \Theta} p(w|\theta_D) p(\theta_D|R = r)$$

and $p(\theta_D|R = r)$ is set to uniform.

$p(\theta_D|w, R = r)$ can be computed as:[3]

$$p(\theta_D|w, R = r) \propto \frac{p(w|\theta_D) p(\theta_D|R = r)}{\sum_{\theta'_D \in \Theta} p(w|\theta'_D) p(\theta'_D|R = r)} .$$

Again, $p(\theta'_D)$ and $p(\theta_D)$ are set to uniform in [71].

Plugging these refinements into the estimate of the relevance model $p(w|Q, R = r)$ and after some algebraic transformation, we can obtain:

$$p(w|Q, R=r) \propto \frac{\sum_{\theta_D \in \Theta} p(w|\theta_D) p(\theta_D|R=r)}{\sum_{\theta'_D \in \Theta} p(w|\theta'_D) p(\theta'_D|R=r)} \prod_{i=1}^{m} \sum_{\theta_D \in \Theta} p(q_i|\theta_D, R = r) p(w|\theta_D) p(\theta_D|R=r)$$

$$= \prod_{i=1}^{m} \sum_{\theta_D \in \Theta} (p(q_i|\theta_D, R=r) p(w|\theta_D) p(\theta_D|R=r)) .$$

Written in this form, the estimate formula is again seen as giving high probabilities to words occurring frequently in those documents that give our query a high likelihood (thus more likely relevant documents). Indeed, if we rewrite the estimate of Model 1 in the following form, we see that the two models mainly differ in how they aggregate the evidence of a word w co-occurring with query words:

$$p(w|Q, R = r) \propto \sum_{\theta_D \in \Theta} \prod_{i=1}^{m} (p(q_i|\theta_D, R = r) p(w|\theta_D) p(\theta_D|R = r)) .$$

In both models, the "co-occurrence evidence" of word w with a query word q_i is captured by the same term $p(q_i|\theta_D, R = r) p(w|\theta_D) p(\theta_D|R = r)$. However, Model 1 first aggregates the evidence for all the query words by taking a product, and then further aggregates the evidence by summing over all the possible document models, while Model 2 does the opposite. In [71], it was reported that Model 2 performs slightly better than Model 1, and Model 2 significantly outperforms the baseline simple query likelihood retrieval model. Relevance model has also later been applied to other tasks such as cross-lingual [147].

Theoretically speaking, the relevance models can be potentially computed over the entire space of empirical document models. However, in the experiments reported in [71], the authors restricted the computation to the top 50 documents returned for each query. This not only improves the efficiency, but also improves the robustness of the estimated model as we are at a lower risk of

---

[3]The formula given in [71]: is $p(M_i|w) = p(w|M_i)p(w)/p(M_i)$, which is probably meant to be $p(M_i|w) = p(w|M_i)p(M_i)/p(w)$; M_i is the same as θ_D.

including some distracting document models. Indeed, as shown in [71], including more documents can be potentially harmful. This is the same observation as in [1], all suggesting that these models are essentially alternative ways of implementing pseudo feedback with language models.

5.3.4   STRUCTURED QUERY MODELS

Sometimes a query may be characterized with multiple aspects and has some structure. This may happen in several cases, including multiple representations of queries or queries formulated based on structured data.

For example, TREC queries are typically described with several fields including a concise title field, a one-sentence description, and a relatively long narrative. These different fields provide a different representation of the same query. A query may also be represented with different granularities of lexical units. For example, one representation may be based on unigrams, and another may be based on word associations extracted from some domain resources [148].

When we formulate a query based on information from multiple fields in a relational database, we would also naturally have a query with multiple fields. For example, a sample query topic in TREC 2003 Genomics Track [149] has the following two fields:

Field 1 (Gene Name): activating transcription factor 2
Field 2 (Gene Symbols): ATF2, HB16

In all these cases, a query is characterized with multiple aspects, which are usually either multiple representations or multiple text fields. When we design a retrieval model for handling such structured queries, presumably we should consider the structure and assign potentially different weights to these different aspects.

Consider the gene query example above. Since a gene symbol uniquely identifies a gene, but a word in the name only partially identifies a gene, intuitively matching a term (i.e., a symbol) in the symbol field is worth more than matching a term in the name field. Indeed, matching a symbol is about equal to matching the entire name phrase. Thus, if we ignore the structure and simply combine all the fields together, the retrieval results would be nonoptimal.

This means that using one single "flat" (unstructured) query language model to represent the query appears to an over-simplification because it does not allow us to flexibly put different weights on different representations or different fields. A better solution would be to define the query model as a mixture model, which has indeed been done in [148] for combining multiple sources of knowledge about query expansion and in [117] for assigning different weights to different fields of a gene query. We call such mixture query language models *structured query models*.

Specifically, let $Q = \{Q_1, ..., Q_k\}$ be a query with k aspects, where Q_i represents a query aspect. The mixture query model can be defined as:

$$p(w|\theta_Q) = \sum_{i=1}^{k} \lambda_i \, p(w|\theta_{Q_i})$$

where $p(w|\theta_{Q_i})$ is a query model corresponding to aspect Q_i, and λ_i is the corresponding weight. The challenge here is to optimize the setting of the weight of each aspect λ_i and estimate each component aspect query language model θ_{Q_i}.

In [117], a pseudo feedback algorithm is proposed to expand each $p(w|\theta_{Q_i})$ and estimate λ_i simultaneously. The basic idea is to use each field (Q_i) to define a prior on θ_{Q_i} and fit the mixture model to a set of feedback documents in the same way as fitting the two-component mixture model for model-based feedback discussed in Section 5.3.1. Once we can estimate these parameters, we can combine the component models to compute a structured query language model $p(w|\theta_Q)$ and use it in the KL-divergence retrieval model for scoring documents. The structured query model estimated using this pseudo feedback technique is shown to be more effective than simply weighting all the fields equally [117].

In [150], how to match such a structured query with *structured* documents is studied. In their problem setup, a query and a document are assumed to have the same number of fields (a common scenario in database record retrieval). The proposed scoring function is a weighted combination of the scores on each field. See Section 6.3 for more discussion about this work and other work on retrieval of structured documents.

5.4   NEGATIVE RELEVANCE FEEDBACK

Most of the query model estimation methods discussed in this chapter can effectively use information in the examples of relevant documents or top-ranked documents that have been assumed to be relevant. We have not discussed how we can learn from examples of nonrelevant documents (i.e., negative examples). Indeed, when a query is very difficult for a system, the first page of initial retrieval results can be all nonrelevant. In such a case, if we want to help the user by improving the ranking of the results on the next page, we would only have negative feedback examples to learn from.

Unfortunately it is nontrivial to use negative information in the KL-divergence retrieval model. The difficulty simply comes from the fact that we use a generative query language model (i.e., θ_Q) to represent the information need, and the model cannot assign a negative probability to any term, making it hard to *penalize* a term. The best we could do is to assign a zero probability to those distracting terms. But if we truncate a query model to keep only the most significant terms, as we often have to do for the sake of efficiency, such a strategy for penalization may not be so effective because many other useful terms also have zero probabilities due to truncation so we cannot really distinguish truly distracting terms from those terms ignored due to truncation.

To solve this problem, a heuristic modification of the KL-divergence retrieval model is proposed in [138]. The basic idea is to introduce a *negative topic language model* θ_N. We could then use θ_N to retrieve documents that are potentially distracting and compute a "distraction score" for each document. The distraction score of a document can then be combined with the original KL-divergence score of the document in such a way that we would penalize a document that has a high distraction score.

The proposed formula for scoring is:

$$Score(Q, D) = -D(\theta_Q || \theta_D) + \beta D(\theta_N || \theta_D) , \qquad (5.3)$$

where β is a parameter that controls the amount of negative feedback. When $\beta = 0$, we do not perform negative feedback, and the ranking would be the same as the original ranking according to θ_Q.

This scoring function can be shown to be equivalent to the following for ranking documents [138]:

$$Score(Q, D) \overset{rank}{=} \sum_{w \in V} [p(w|\theta_Q) - \beta p(w|\theta_N)] \log p(w|\theta_D) .$$

In this new form of the scoring formula, we see that each term has a weight of $[p(w|\theta_Q) - \beta p(w|\theta_N)] \log p(w|\theta_D)$, which penalizes a term that has high probability according to the negative topic model θ_N. Thus, the negative feedback model is essentially very similar to Rocchio in the vector space model and can in some sense be regarded as the language modeling version of Rocchio.

The negative query model θ_N can be estimated based on negative feedback documents in the same way as a regular positive query model would be estimated based on positive feedback documents (e.g., using the two-component mixture model discussed in Section 5.3.1). Since a query term tends to occur frequently in the top-ranked negative documents, it may have a high probability according to θ_N, which is not what we want. To solve this problem, in [138], the authors heuristically let θ_N assign zero probabilities to all the query terms. Furthermore, since negative documents generally do not form a coherent cluster, it may be more effective to learn multiple negative models from a set of negative feedback documents and penalize a document close to *any* of the negative models. Such a strategy has been shown to be more effective than using a single negative feedback model [151]. In [151], it is also shown that language models are more effective than the vector-space model for pure negative feedback with no relevant examples.

Note that negative feedback can be more naturally done in the classical probabilistic model (e.g., [56]) because they can be used directly to improve the estimate of the nonrelevant document model $p(D|Q, R = \bar{r})$. Thus, if we use multinomial distributions to model documents in a classical probabilistic retrieval model, we can easily use relevance model to estimate $p(D|Q, R = r)$, and at the same time use negative feedback documents to improve our estimate of $p(D|Q, R = \bar{r})$, which would otherwise have to be estimated based on the approximation of nonrelevant documents with the entire collection. However, no experiment results in this direction have been reported yet.

5.5   SUMMARY

In this chapter, we discussed probabilistic distance retrieval models and how feedback (particularly pseudo feedback) can be performed with language models. As a generalization of query likelihood scoring, the KL-divergence retrieval model has now been established as the state of the art approach for using language models to rank documents. It supports all kinds of feedback through estimating a query language model based on feedback information. We reviewed several different approaches to improving the estimation of a query language model by using word co-occurrences in the corpus. Although some approaches are meant to work on the entire corpus, they tend to work much better when restricting the estimation to using only the top-ranked documents. Thus, it is fair to say that all these methods are essentially different ways to implement the traditional pseudo feedback heuristic with language models. Among all the methods, the two-component mixture model [134, 139] and the relevance model [71] appear to be most effective and robust and also are computationally feasible. The success of these feedback methods shows that we can generally improve retrieval performance by improving the estimate of a language model or improving the design of language models for retrieval. This is a significant advantage of the language modeling approach over the traditional vector space model, where we have little guidance on how to improve an existing model.

We have also discussed the difficulty in performing negative feedback with a probabilistic distance retrieval model and a heuristic extension of the KL-divergence retrieval model so that it can effectively perform negative feedback in a way similar to how Rocchio handles negative feedback in the traditional vector-space model.

CHAPTER 6

Language Models for Special Retrieval Tasks

In addition to their applications to the standard monolingual ad hoc search problem, language models have also been applied to solve many other "nonstandard" retrieval problems, including cross-lingual retrieval, distributed IR, expert finding, personalized search, modeling redundancy, passage retrieval, subtopic retrieval, and topic detection and tracking, among others. Most of these additional applications share the same philosophy as the language models developed for the standard ad hoc retrieval problem in modeling text generally with probabilistic models and leveraging statistical estimation methods to tune and optimize weights.

In this chapter, we will review some of the major work in this line with an emphasis on applications of language models in *unsupervised* settings (as opposed to settings involving *supervised* learning) and applications where interesting *extensions* of the standard ad hoc retrieval models have been made (as opposed to where a standard language model is applied to an application in a straightforward way). We have intentionally left out work on using language models in *supervised* learning settings, where labeled training data is needed, because the latter, which includes many important tasks such as text categorization [39, 66], information filtering [152], and topic tracking and detection [153, 120, 154], is better reviewed through comparing the generative language models with many other competing supervised or semi-supervised learning methods, notably discriminative approaches such as Support Vector Machines [155].

6.1 CROSS-LINGUAL INFORMATION RETRIEVAL

Cross-lingual information retrieval (CLIR) refers to the task of retrieving documents in one language (e.g., English) with a query in another language (e.g., Chinese). A major challenge in cross-lingual IR is to cross the language barrier in some way, typically involving translating either the query or the document from one language to the other.

The translation model discussed in Section 4.5 can be naturally applied to solve this problem by defining the translation probability $p(u|v)$ on terms in the two languages involved in the retrieval task. For example, let v be a word in English and u a word in Chinese. In such a case, $p(u|v)$ would give us the probability that u is a good translation of English word v in Chinese, thus it captures the semantic association between words in different languages.

This idea has been applied to CLIR in [156] and [130], but these two studies used the translation model in a slightly different way. In both studies, the basic retrieval function is the query likelihood retrieval model. That is, the score of a document D in a target language (e.g., English) with respect to a query $Q = q_1...q_m$ in a source language (e.g., Chinese) is given by:

$$p(Q|D) = \prod_{i=1}^{m} p(q_i|\theta_D^S)$$

where the distribution $p(.|\theta_D^S)$ is a language model in *source* language estimated based on document D (note that D is in the *target* language).

Suppose $p(u|v)$ is a translation model estimated using resources such as parallel corpora or bilingual dictionaries, where u and v are in our source and target languages, respectively. That is, $p(u|v)$ encodes our knowledge about how to translate a word in the target language (v) into one in the source language (u). In both [156] and [130], $p(q_i|\theta_D^S)$ is computed using a variant of the following formula:

$$p(q_i|\theta_D^S) = \sum_{w \in V_T} p(q_i|w)p(w|\theta_D^T)$$

where V_T is the vocabulary set of the target language and the distribution $p(.|\theta_D^T)$ is a target language model estimated based on D.

As in the case of monolingual query likelihood scoring, we need to smooth the document language model (either θ_D^S or θ_D^T or both), and this is where the two studies differ. In [156], only θ_D^T (but not θ_D^S) is smoothed with the target language document collection C_T. That is, the actual formula for computing $p(q_i|\theta_D^S)$ is:

$$p(q_i|\theta_D^S) = \sum_{w \in V_T} p(q_i|w)[(1 - \lambda_T)p(w|\theta_D^T) + \lambda_T p(w|C_T)]$$

where λ_T is a smoothing parameter. In [130], the authors did the opposite: they smoothed only θ_D^S, but not θ_D^T. Their actual formula for computing $p(q_i|\theta_D^S)$ is:

$$p(q_i|\theta_D^S) = [(1 - \lambda_S) \sum_{w \in V_T} p(q_i|w)p(w|\theta_D^T)] + \lambda_S p(w|C_S)]$$

where λ_S is a smoothing parameter and C_S denotes a source text collection to be used as a reference corpus for smoothing.

As in the translation model for monolingual ad hoc retrieval, a major challenge here is to estimate the translation probability $p(q_i|w)$. In both [156] and [130], the authors experimented with several options for estimating this translation model, such as using a bilingual word list, parallel corpora, and a combination of them. In general, the cross-lingual query likelihood retrieval function has been shown to be effective (e.g., achieving over 85% performance of monolingual retrieval baseline in [130]). In [156], different disambiguation methods to resolve translation ambiguity are also studied. Their conclusion is that lexical disambiguation appears to be non essential for cross-lingual retrieval, and using all the possible translations performs the best.

In another line of work on applying language models to CLIR, Lavrenko et al. [147] adapted the relevance model (discussed in detail in Section 5.3.3) in two ways to perform CLIR, both based on the KL-divergence scoring function instead of the query likelihood retrieval function which is used in the work discussed above. The document language model θ_D is estimated in a normal way, thus it assigns probabilities to words in the target language. Their main idea is to adapt relevance model so that we can start with a query Q in the *source* language to estimate a query model θ_Q that can assign probabilities to words in the *target* language. This way, the query model and the document model would be in the same language (i.e., target language), so they can be compared using the KL-divergence scoring function to computed a score for retrieval.

Their first method is to leverage a parallel corpus where documents in the source language are paired with translations of them in the target language. In this case, the document model θ_D in their relevance model can be generalized to include two separate models, one for each language. That is, $\theta_D = (\theta_D^S, \theta_D^T)$ where θ_D^S is the model for the source document and θ_D^T the model for the corresponding target document. With this setup, the relevance model can be generalized in a straightforward way to give the following probability of word w^T in the target language according to the query model θ_Q:

$$p(w^T|\theta_Q) \propto \sum_{\theta_D \in \Theta} p(\theta_D) p(w^T|\theta_D^T) \prod_{i=1}^{m} p(q_i|\theta_D^S)$$

where $Q = q_1...q_m$ is the query.

We see that the estimated target language model for the query $p(w^T|\theta_Q)$ would assign a high probability to a word frequent in a target document whose translation document in the source language matches our query well (i.e., the likelihood $\prod_{i=1}^{m} p(q_i|\theta_D^S)$ is high). The pairing of θ_D^S and θ_D^T has enabled the crossing of the language barrier.

Their second method is to leverage a bilingual dictionary to induce a translation model $p(w^S|w^T)$ and use this translation model to convert the document language model $p(w^T|\theta_D)$, which is in the target language, to a document language model for the source language $p(w^S|\theta_D)$. That is:

$$p(w^T|\theta_Q) \quad \propto \quad \sum_{\theta_D \in \Theta} p(\theta_D) p(w^T|\theta_D) \prod_{i=1}^{m} p(q_i^S|\theta_D) \tag{6.1}$$

$$= \quad \sum_{\theta_D \in \Theta} p(\theta_D) p(w^T|\theta_D) \prod_{i=1}^{m} \sum_{u^T \in V^T} p(q_i^S|u^T) p(u^T|\theta_D) . \tag{6.2}$$

This time, the translation model $p(q_i^S|u^T)$ has enabled the crossing of the language barrier.

These models have been shown to achieve very good retrieval performance (90–95% of a strong monolingual baseline).

6.2 DISTRIBUTED INFORMATION RETRIEVAL

Distributed information retrieval is concerned with retrieving information from multiple collections of documents that may be physically or logically distributed among multiple machines in a network. The task of distributed IR can often be decomposed into two subtasks: (1) resource selection; and (2) result fusion. Given a query, the task of resource selection is to select the resources (i.e., collections) that most likely contain relevant documents to the query. With resource selection, we can then execute the query only on these most promising resources to improve efficiency. The task of result fusion is to combine the search results from multiple sources to generate an integrated set of results for the query. Language models have been applied to both tasks.

For resource selection, the general idea is to treat each collection as a special "document" and apply standard language models to rank collections. In an early work by Xu and Croft [135], the authors cluster the documents to form topical clusters. Each cluster is then treated as one coherent subcollection, which is then used to estimate a topic language model. The KL-divergence between the empirical query word distribution and the estimated topic language model is then used to select the most promising topical collections for further querying. Such a clustering method is shown to be effective for collection selection [135].

In [157], the authors proposed a language modeling framework for resource selection and result fusion. In this framework, documents in each collection are scored using regular query likelihood retrieval function but smoothed with the background language model corresponding to the collection. As a result, the scores of documents in different collections are strictly speaking not comparable because of the use of different background language model for smoothing. A major contribution of the work [157] is to derive an adjustment strategy that can ensure that the scores of all the documents would be comparable after adjustment.

Specifically, let D be a document in collection C_i. In general, we would score a document for query Q with query likelihood and rank documents based on $p(Q|D, C_i)$. The likelihood is conditioned on C_i because of smoothing, thus directly merging results based on their query likelihood scores $p(Q|D, C_i)$ would be problematic since the scores may not be comparable. Thus, the authors of [157] use probabilistic rules to derive a normalized form of the likelihood denoted as $p(Q|D)$, which can then be used as scores of documents for the purpose of result fusion. They show that ranking based on $p(Q|D)$ is equivalent to ranking based on $\frac{p(Q|D,C_i)}{\beta p(C_i|Q)+1}$, where β is a parameter to be empirically set. Thus, when we merge the results, we just need to divide the original score $p(Q|D, C_i)$ by the normalizer $\beta p(C_i|Q) + 1$, which can be computed using Bayes rule and the likelihood of the query given collection C_i (i.e., $p(Q|C_i)$). Their experiment results show that this language modeling approach is effective for distributed IR and outperforms a state of the art method (i.e., CORI [158]) [157].

6.3   STRUCTURED DOCUMENT RETRIEVAL AND COMBINING REPRESENTATIONS

Most retrieval models are designed to work on a bag of words representation of a document, thus they ignore any structure of a document. In reality, there often exist both intra-document structures (e.g., title vs. body) and inter-document structures (e.g., hyperlinks and topical relations) that can be potentially leveraged to improve search accuracy. This is especially true in XML retrieval and Web search. It is also common that one may obtain multiple text representations of the same document, which should be combined to improve retrieval accuracy. These multiple representations can also be regarded as multiple "parts" of a document, thus giving an intra-document structure.

In exploiting intra-document structures, we generally assume that a document D has k parts or k text representations $D = \{D_1, ..., D_k\}$, and our goal is to rank such documents with consideration of the known structure of the document. In Ogilvie and Callan [159], the authors have extended the basic query likelihood to address this problem. Their approach allows different parts of a document or different representations of a document to be combined with different weights. Specifically, the "generation" process of a query given a document is assumed to consist of two steps. In the first step, a part D_i is selected from the structured document D according to a selection probability $p(D_i|D)$. In the second, a query is generated using the selected part D_i. Thus, the query likelihood is given by:

$$p(Q|\theta_D) = \prod_{i=1}^{m} p(q_i|\theta_D) \tag{6.3}$$

$$= \prod_{i=1}^{m} \sum_{j=1}^{k} p(q_i|\theta_{D_j}) p(D_j|D) . \tag{6.4}$$

In [159], such a two-step generation process was not explicitly given, but their model implies such a generation process. The "part selection probability" $p(D_i|D)$ is denoted by λ_i in [159]; it can be interpreted as the weight assigned to D_i and can be set based on prior knowledge or estimated using training data. Experiment results show that this language modeling approach to combining multiple representations is effective. Language models have also been applied to XML retrieval by other researchers [160].

An alternative way of modeling structured document retrieval (with structured queries) is presented in [150], where the authors applied the relevance model to score each field (or representation) of a document separately and then combine the scores linearly. Specifically, in their setup, the query is also assumed to contain k fields, corresponding to the k fields in the documents. Thus, we may denote a query by $Q = \{Q_1, ..., Q_k\}$ (see Section 5.3.4 for more discussion about retrieval with structured queries). Suppose θ_{Q_i} is an estimated relevance model for the i-th field. The proposed scoring function is:

$$Score(Q, D) = \sum_{i=k} \lambda_i \sum_{w \in V} p(w|\theta_{Q_i}) \log p(w|\theta_{D_i})$$

where λ_i is a weighting parameter for the i-th field. We see that this is basically to first score each field using cross entropy (equivalently KL-divergence) and then combine these "field scores." An interesting question studied in this work is how to infer missing values of some fields in the structured documents (the documents are database records with text fields in [150]). The idea of their solution is to infer a missing value in a record based on its context in that record (i.e., other fields with known values).

Inter-document structures are usually exploited through propagating information through the structural links among documents. A general probabilistic propagation framework was proposed in [161] to combine probabilistic content-based retrieval models (including language models) with link structures (e.g., hyperlinks). The basic idea is to first compute content-based scores for all the documents in a hypertext collection and then probabilistically propagate these scores through hyperlinks so that the score of a document would be iteratively adjusted based on the scores of its neighboring documents. Experiment results show that the propagation framework can improve ranking accuracy over pure content-based scoring. While this probabilistic propagation framework is not specific to language models, it was shown in [161] that the performance is much better if the content-based scores can be interpreted as probabilities of relevance. Another general (non-probabilistic) propagation framework was proposed in [162] which has been shown to be effective for improving Web search through both score propagation and term count propagation. How to integrate such propagation frameworks with language models more tightly remains an interesting future research question.

6.4   PERSONALIZED AND CONTEXT-SENSITIVE SEARCH

In the "standard" setup of the retrieval task (and most search engine systems), we generally assume that the query is the only information we have available about a user. Unfortunately a query is often very short and not very informative. In personalized search, we would like to use more user information to better infer a user's information need. Such information can include, e.g., the entire search history of a user, which is naturally available to a retrieval system. Users with similar information needs can also benefit from sharing their search histories to improve search results, though privacy infringement may be a concern [163].

Since even the same user may use similar queries (e.g., an ambiguous query) to find different information, it is very important for a retrieval system to adapt in real-time to recognize the *current* information need of a user. Thus, the immediate search context in the current search session, such as which documents in the search results are viewed and which are skipped, is extremely valuable for inferring a user's interest.

With language models, we may achieve the goal of personalized and context-sensitive search by estimating a better query language model with all the available user information and search context. Normally, we estimate a query model θ_Q based on the query Q and possibly feedback documents in the current collection C. In personalized search, we would have additional information from the user that can be exploited. We use U to denote *all* the information from the current user, which may include, e.g., past queries, viewed documents, and skipped documents in the search history (particularly the current search session), and other user factors that may affect our inference of the user's information need. Formally, we would like to compute:

$$\hat{\theta}_Q = \arg\max_{\theta} p(\theta|Q, C, U) .$$

Using such a strategy, in [164, 165], the authors proposed several methods for improving the estimate of a query language model based on implicit feedback information (e.g., the previous queries and clickthroughs of a user). These methods are shown to be effective for improving search accuracy for a new related query.

In [164], implicit feedback within a single search session is considered. This is to simulate a scenario when the initial search results were not satisfactory to the user, so the user would reformulate the query potentially multiple times. The feedback information available consists of the previous queries and the snippets of viewed documents (i.e., clickthrough information). Given the user's current query, the question is how to use such feedback information to improve the estimate of the query language model θ_Q. In [164], four different methods were proposed to solve this problem, all essentially leading to some interpolation of many unigram language models estimated using different feedback information, respectively. Different methods mainly differ in the way to assign weights to different types of information (e.g., queries vs. snippets).

Experiment results show that using the history information, especially the snippets of viewed documents, can improve search accuracy for the current query. It is also shown to be beneficial to use a dynamic interpolation coefficient similar to Dirichlet prior smoothing. In particular, the following simple Dirichlet prior interpolation is shown to work well:

$$p(w\theta_Q) = \frac{c(w, Q) + \mu p(w|H_Q) + \nu p(w|H_C)}{|Q| + \mu + \nu}$$

where H_Q and H_C are the set of previous queries and the set of the snippets of viewed documents (called clickthroughs) in the current session, respectively. μ and ν are two parameters to control the weight assigned to the query history and the clickthrough history, respectively. In the experiments reported in [164], the optimal values for μ and ν were $\mu = 0.2$ and $\nu = 5.0$, suggesting that the query history is roughly worth 0.2 "pseudo query word," while the clickthrough history is worth much more (roughly 5 query words). Note that with fixed μ and ν, a shorter query would be more influenced by the history information than a longer query, which is intuitively reasonably as we would have more confidence on the current query if it is long.

In [165], implicit feedback using the entire (long-term) search history of a user is considered. Since in this setup, there is potentially noisy information in the search history, it is important to filter out such noise when estimating the query language model. The idea presented in [165] for solving this problem is the following: First, each past query is treated as a unit and represented by the snippets of the top-ranked search results. Second, the search results (snippets) of the current query is used to assign a weight to each past query based on the similarity between the search results of the past query and those of the current one. The weighting helps filter out any noisy information in the history. Finally, the query language model is estimated as a weighted combination of unigram language models estimated based on text associated with each past query (e.g., query text, clicked snippets). The second step above is implemented by using a mixture model with each past query contributing a component language model to fit the current search results. The EM algorithm is used to compute the ML estimate so that we can obtain optimal weights for all the past queries. Intuitively, the weight of each past query indicates how well the search results of that query can explain the current search results, i.e., similarity between that past query and the current query. Evaluation shows that such a language modeling approach to query estimation based on search history can improve performance substantially [165].

The work discussed above all essentially performs implicit feedback, which does not require any extra effort from the user. If, however, a user is willing to provide some explicit feedback (as, e.g., in the case of a difficult topic or a high-recall retrieval task), personalization can be more effectively achieved through explicit relevance feedback, and the techniques discussed in Section 5.3 can be used to improve our estimate of the query language model based on feedback documents. Unfortunately, relevance feedback would not work if the initial search results are so poor that none of the top-ranked documents is relevant. In such a case, term-based feedback may be useful. A language modeling approach to term-based feedback is described in [166], where the feedback terms are not only directly used in constructing an improved query language model, but also used to infer the weights of some underlying topic clusters, allowing us to effectively further expand the query model with additional terms in highly weighted clusters (i.e., combining explicit term feedback with pseudo feedback). Experiment results show that it is beneficial to combine three kinds of terms: the original query terms, new feedback terms, and additional terms from the top-ranked documents [166].

6.5 EXPERT FINDING

The task of expert finding as set up in the TREC Enterprise Track is the following: Given a list of names and emails of candidate experts and text collections where their expertise may be mentioned, retrieve experts with expertise on a given topic (described by keywords). Language models have been applied to this task with reasonable success [167, 168].

In [167], a general probabilistic model is presented for solving this problem with an analogous derivation to the one given in [55]. Specifically, three random variables are introduced: (1) T for topic; (2) C for a candidate expert; (3) $R \in \{0, 1\}$ for relevance. The goal is to rank the candidates according to the conditional probability $p(R = 1|T, C)$. Following the derivation in [55], the authors derived two families of models corresponding to two different ways of factoring the joint probability $p(T, C|R)$, either as $p(T|R, C)p(C|R)$, which is called topic generation model or $p(C|T, R)p(T|R)$, which is called candidate generation model.

Specifically, after some similar transformations to those discussed in Section 2.2, the two families of general expert finding models are:

Topic generation model:

$$p(R = 1|T, C) \stackrel{\text{rank}}{=} \frac{p(C|R = 1)}{p(C|R = 0)} \times \frac{p(T|C, R = 1)}{p(T|C, R = 0)} \; .$$

$p(C|R = 1)$ and $p(C|R = 0)$ can be regarded as our prior about whether C is likely an expert on any topic, while $p(T|C, R = 1)$ and $p(T|C, R = 0)$ can be interpreted as characterizing the expertise of candidate C, and they can be estimated using documents describing the expertise of candidates such as technical email messages from/to a candidate.

Candidate generation model:

$$p(R = 1|T, C) \stackrel{\text{rank}}{=} \frac{p(C|T, R = 1)}{p(C|T, R = 0)} \; .$$

Intuitively, $p(C|T, R = 1)$ is the probability that C is an expert on topic T, while $p(C|T, R = 0)$ is the probability that C is *not* an expert on T. However, we do not generally have the data that would allow us to estimate these models directly (or otherwise, the problem of expert finding would have been trivial). Thus, again we have to rely on data such as technical email messages from/to a candidate to infer these models, and there are multiple ways of doing this.

In [167], the authors proposed three techniques to improve the estimation of these models: (1) a mixture model for modeling the candidate mentions, which can effectively assign different weights to different representations of an expert; (2) topic expansion to enrich topic representation; and (3) email-based candidate prior to prefer candidates with many email mentions. These techniques are shown to be empirically effective.

In [168], the authors proposed two different topic generation models for expert finding. In both models, we would leverage the co-occurrences of terms referring to a candidate and terms describing a topic in some text documents to estimate p(T|C,R=1). However, the two models differ in the way a topic T is "generated" from a candidate C. In Model 1, a topic is generated by generating each word in the topic *independently*, thus the generation of two words of the topic can potentially be going through a different document, and a bridge document only needs to match the candidate and *one* topic word well. In Model 2, the whole topic is generated together using the same document as a bridge, thus requiring the bridge document to match both the candidate and the *entire* topic well. Intuitively, Model 2 appears to be more reasonable than Model 1. Indeed, empirical experiments also show that Model 2 outperforms Model 1 [168]. This is a case where some analysis of the assumptions made in designing language models can help assess the effectiveness of a model for retrieval.

6.6   PASSAGE RETRIEVAL

A standard retrieval system returns a whole document as a unit of search results for a query. However, it often happens that only a part of a document is relevant to a query. In such a case, a user would need to read the entire document to locate the most relevant passage. Also, in a network retrieval system where transfer of information incurs cost, sending an entire document to a user consumes much more resource than sending just a relevant passage. Thus, it is often desirable to return directly the relevant passages in response to a query. This is called passage retrieval.

Generally speaking, there are two strategies for passage retrieval: (1) pre-segment documents into overlapping or nonoverlapping segments and treat each segment as if it were a document; (2) extract relevant passages dynamically for a given query. The former is more efficient at retrieval time, but has the disadvantage that the granularity of passages must be fixed in advance. The latter is precisely the opposite: we can dynamically determine the boundary of a relevant passage based on the query which is desirable since the lengths of relevant passages may vary dramatically from queries to queries, but it is computationally more expensive at retrieval time.

Language models have been applied to perform passage retrieval in both ways. In [115], the standard KL-divergence retrieval model is applied to perform passage retrieval with various strategies for pre-segmentation of passages. The results show that language models are applicable to passage retrieval and can achieve better or comparable performance as compared with the baseline method of using full text. Furthermore, passage retrieval based on language models appears to be beneficial for applying relevance models to do pseudo feedback, likely because the top-ranked small passages have less noise than the top-ranked full documents.

In [169], a hidden Markov model (HMM) is applied to dynamically identify the boundaries of a relevant passage in a long document based on a given query. Hidden Markov Models [170] are a special kind of language models that can model the underlying *latent* structures of a sequence of words. The architecture of the HMM used in [169] is shown in Figure 6.1. It models a text document with one single relevant passage with five states, including a special state to align with the end of the document (state E). The other four states are to model background words before the relevant passage (state $B1$), query-related words within the relevant passage (state R), background words within the relevant passage (state $B2$), and background words after the relevant passage (state $B3$), respectively. The output distribution of all the background states is set to the collection language model. The output distribution of state R can be regarded as a query language model or relevance model. It can be estimated based on the original query, and improved through using various kinds of pseudo feedback techniques [169]. Experiment results show that this HMM can accurately identify relevant passages of variable lengths from long documents.

6.7   SUBTOPIC RETRIEVAL

The subtopic retrieval task represents an interesting retrieval task because it requires modeling the *dependency* of relevance of individual documents [91]. Given a topic query, the task of subtopic retrieval is to retrieve documents that can cover as many subtopics of the topic as possible. For example, a student doing a literature survey on machine learning may want to find documents that cover representative approaches to machine learning. Thus, he/she may use a query like "representative machine learning methods" to attempt to retrieve documents that can cover as many different machine learning methods as possible. That is, the result set should be as diverse as possible, and a

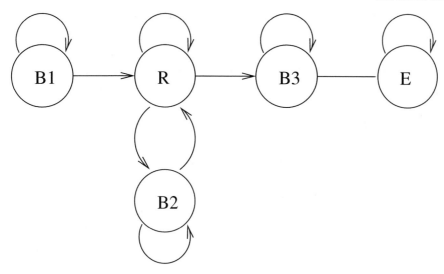

Figure 6.1:   An HMM for extracting coherent relevant passages.

document covering multiple machine learning methods should be ranked above those that just cover one single method.

If we are to solve the problem with a traditional retrieval model, we likely would have a great deal of redundancy in the top ranked documents. As a result, although most top-ranked documents may be relevant to the query, they may all cover just one subtopic, thus we do not end up having a high coverage of subtopics. For example, with a standard search engine, the query above may give us many documents about a popular learning method such as SVM on the top. This is because the relevance status of each document is evaluated *separately*, but for this task, we must consider the dependency among the results.

Intuitively, we may solve this problem by attempting to remove the redundancy in the search results, hoping that by avoiding covering already covered subtopics, we will have a higher chance of covering new subtopics quickly. This is precisely the idea explored in [91] where the authors used a novelty measure to be discussed in Section 6.8.1 in combination with the query likelihood relevance scoring to iteratively select the best document that is both relevant and is different from the already picked documents. Such a greedy ranking strategy is often called maximal marginal relevance (MMR) ranking, and was first proposed in [171].

The MMR strategy for subtopic retrieval optimizes the coverage of subtopics *indirectly* through avoiding repeatedly covering the same subtopics. A more direct way to optimize the coverage of subtopics is to model the possible subtopics in the documents through topic models such as Probabilistic Latent Semantic Indexing (PLSI) [32] or Latent Dirichlet Allocation (LDA) [172], and rank documents so as to maximize the coverage of subtopics jointly achieved by all the documents. (PLSA and LDA will be discussed in more detail in Chapter 7.) A greedy algorithm similar to MMR can be used to gradually select documents that can offer complementary coverage of subtopics with those already selected documents. This strategy has been studied in [89] and later adapted to solve the review assignment problem in [173]. While intuitively appealing, the preliminary results of this strategy appear to be not as good as those of the MMR strategy [89]. One possible reason may be that when a document and a query are matched based on their low-dimensional representation in the topic space, we lack the needed level of discrimination which we would have when we represent them in the original term space. Thus, if may be possible to combine such a subtopic representation with word-level representation to improve the performance (see Section 7.5 for more discussion about this point). Clearly more work needs to be done to better understand these methods.

The subtopic retrieval problem also poses challenges in evaluation because the traditional measures such as precision and recall cannot be used directly for evaluating subtopic retrieval results. In [91], the authors proposed two new measures called *subtopic precision* and *subtopic recall*, which can be regarded as a generalization of the standard precision and recall. Furthermore, to penalize redundancy among the results, they further generalized subtopic precision to define a weighted subtopic precision. Both subtopic precision and weighted subtopic precision are normalized with their best values achieved with an ideal ranking of results to address the variances in the intrinsic difficulty of different queries. Such a normalization strategy has also been used in defining NDCG to measure the accuracy of regular retrieval results [8].

6.8   OTHER RETRIEVAL-RELATED TASKS

6.8.1   MODELING REDUNDANCY AND NOVELTY

A basic task in many applications is to measure the redundancy between two documents often for the purpose of removing or reducing the redundancy in some way. For example, we may want to reduce redundancy in search results. A somewhat equivalent, but complementary, problem with redundancy measurement is to measure the novelty of a document in the context of another document or a set of documents, also with many applications. For example, detecting the first news story about an event has been a major task in the Topic Detection and Tracking (TDT) initiative [174].

Language models can be used to solve this problem in several ways. One way is to compute the cross-entropy (or KL-divergence) between two document language models to obtain asymmetric similarities (see, e.g., [175, 43, 175, 113]). This approach is essentially to take one document as a "query" and score the other document with respect to this query using a retrieval function. For example, the following approach is proposed in [113]:

Let $\theta_{D_1}^{MLE}$ be the ML estimate of the document language model for D_1 and $\theta_{D_2}^{\mu}$ be a smoothed document language model for D_2 with Dirichlet prior smoothing (μ is a smoothing parameter). Then we can compute the following asymmetric similarity between these two documents based on the KL-divergence measure:

$$sim(D_1, D_2) = exp(-D(\theta_{D_1}^{MLE}||\theta_{D_2}^{\mu})) \, .$$

This similarity can be interpreted as the redundancy of D_1 w.r.t. D_2. In [113], this method was used to construct a directed document similarity graph.

Another way is to use a mixture language model. For example, in [89, 91], a simple two-component mixture model is used to measure the redundancy (or equivalently novelty) of a document D_1 w.r.t. another document D_2. The idea is to assume that the redundancy of D_1 w.r.t. D_2 corresponds to how well we can predict the content of D_1 using a language model estimated based on D_2. Intuitively, if D_1 is very similar to D_2, then we should expect the model based on D_2 to predict D_1 well (i.e., give high probability to D_1), whereas if they are quite different, the model would not predict D_1 well.

Formally, let θ_{D_2} be a language model estimated using D_2, we define the redundancy of D_1 w.r.t. D_2 as

$$\hat{\lambda} = \underset{\lambda}{\arg\max} \ \log p(D_1|\lambda, \theta_{D_2}) \tag{6.5}$$

$$= \underset{\lambda}{\arg\max} \sum_{w \in V} c(w, D_1) \log(\lambda p(w|\theta_{D_2}) + (1 - \lambda)p(w|C)), \tag{6.6}$$

where $p(w|C)$ is a background collection language model.

Essentially, this is to let the background model and θ_{D_2} to compete for explaining D_1, and $\hat{\lambda} \in [0, 1]$ indicates the relative "competitiveness" of θ_{D_2} to the background model, thus intuitively captures the redundancy. $\hat{\lambda}$ can be computed using the EM algorithm. The novelty can be defined as $1 - \hat{\lambda}$.

A similar but slightly more sophisticated three-component mixture model was proposed in [176] in order to capture novelty in information filtering.

One advantage of this mixture model approach is that the redundancy and novel values are within the same range [0, 1] across all document pairs. If $\hat{\lambda} = 0$, it would mean θ_{D_2} is no better than $p(w|C)$ at all for modeling D_1, thus D_1 can be assumed to have a lot of novel information that does not exist in D_2. At the other extreme, if $\hat{\lambda} = 1$, it would mean θ_{D_2} can explain D_1 very well with no help from $p(w|C)$, thus D_1 does not contain new information that does not exist in D_2, i.e., D_1 is redundant with respect to D_2.

We see that in both approaches, the redundancy/novelty measure is asymmetric in the sense that if we switch the roles of D_1 and D_2, the redundancy value would be different. This is reasonable as, in general, redundancy is asymmetric. For example, if document D_1 is identical to a part of document D_2, D_1 would add no additional information on top of D_2, thus we can say that D_1 is completely redundant with respect to D_2. However, in such a case, it would still be desirable to show D_2 to the user even if the user has already seen D_1 because D_2 can add new information on top of D_1.

Note that these redundancy/novelty measures can also be generalized to measure the redundancy/novelty on multiple documents through aggregation of pairwise redundancy/novelty measures [91].

6.8.2   PREDICTING QUERY DIFFICULTY

Yet another use of language models is to predict query difficulty [177]. The idea is to compare the query model and the collection language model; a query would be assumed to be difficult if its query model is close to the collection language model. The assumption made here is that a discriminative query tends to be easier, and the discriminativeness of a query can be measured by the KL-divergence of the query model and the collection model.

Specifically, a measure called "query clarity" is defined in [177] as follows:

$$clarity(Q) = \sum_{w \in V} p(w|\theta_Q) \log \frac{p(w|\theta_Q)}{p(w|C)} \, ,$$

where θ_Q is usually an expanded query model using any feedback-based query model estimation method (e.g., mixture model [134] or relevance model [71]). We see that this is essentially the KL-divergence of the query model θ_Q and the collection language model $p(w|C)$. Positive correlation between the clarity scores and retrieval accuracy has been observed [177].

6.9   SUMMARY

In this chapter, we reviewed some representative work on applying statistical language models to a variety of special retrieval tasks including cross-language retrieval, distributed information retrieval, structured document retrieval, personalized and context-sensitive retrieval, expert retrieval, passage retrieval, and subtopic retrieval. In all these cases, we have seen that language models can be easily adapted or extended to handle the special needs of an application task. We also discussed the application of language models for some additional retrieval-related tasks, including redundancy removal, novelty detection, and query difficulty prediction. These applications further show the potential of language models for novel applications.

CHAPTER 7

Language Models for Latent Topic Analysis

The language models we have introduced in the previous chapters are mainly designed for the search task, i.e., to generate a ranked list of documents in response to a query. In this chapter, we introduce a family of language models that mainly aim at extracting latent topics from text and performing latent semantic analysis. They are often called probabilistic (statistical) topic models, and can enhance a retrieval system in many ways: First, they enable a low-dimension semantic representation of text, which can potentially improve a retrieval model in two ways: (1) it allows different words capturing the same semantic concept to match each other; and (2) it provides orthogonal and independent semantic dimensions for representing text. Second, they can be used to summarize search results through revealing the major topics in the results, and provide an overview of the results.

This line of work started with the Probabilistic Latent Semantic Analysis (PLSA) model proposed by Hofmann in 1999 [178, 32]. The model can be applied to an arbitrary set of documents to learn a set of latent topic models, each being represented by a word distribution (i.e., unigram language model). In [32], Hofmann shows that representing documents in this latent semantic space, where each dimension corresponds to a latent topic model, can supplement the representation of documents in the original term space to improve retrieval accuracy.

Strictly speaking, however, PLSA is not a generative language model in the sense that it can not be generalized to "generate" new documents because the topic selection probability distribution is associated with a particular document, thus it is not generalizable. To turn PLSA into a true generative model, Blei et al. [172] proposed Latent Dirichlet Allocation (LDA), in which this topic selection distribution would be drawn from a Dirichlet distribution. With LDA, we can potentially draw a different multinomial topic selection distribution for each document, thus the model can easily generate a new document by simply drawing a new topic selection distribution from the trained Dirichlet distribution. Because of this regularization, LDA also solves another problem of PLSA—too many parameters to estimate.

There has been much work to further extend PLSA and LDA mainly to introduce various structures or constraints into the model. We will first introduce the two basic topic models, PLSA and LDA, and then briefly discuss their extensions.

7.1   PROBABILISTIC LATENT SEMANTIC ANALYSIS (PLSA)

The basic idea of PLSA is the following: We assume that there are k latent topics in a set of documents, and each topic would be represented using a word distribution, or a unigram language model, θ_i ($i = 1, ..., k$). We further assume that the words in a document are generated by sampling words independently from a mixture of these k topic models. That is, when we generate a word in document D, we would first choose one of the k topic models according to a topic selection probability distribution $\{p(i|D)\}_{i=1}^{k}$, where $p(i|D)$ is the probability of choosing θ_i, and then sample a word according to the chosen word distribution. Thus, the probability of generating word w in document D would be

$$p_D(w) = \sum_{i=1}^{k} p(i|D)p(w|\theta_i)$$

and the log-likelihood of generating all the words in D would be

$$\log p(D) = \sum_{w \in V} c(w, D) \log \sum_{i=1}^{k} p(i|D)p(w|\theta_i) \, .$$

We typically fit such a model to a collection of documents to discover the exact word distributions of the k latent topics. Formally, let $C = \{D_1, ..., D_{|C|}\}$ be a collection of documents. Clearly, the log-likelihood of the collection is

$$\log p(C|\Lambda) = \sum_{D \in C} \sum_{w \in V} c(w, D) \log \sum_{i=1}^{k} p(i|D)p(w|\theta_i)$$

where Λ denotes the set of all parameters, i.e., $\Lambda = \{p(i|D)\}_{i \in [1,k], D \in C} \cup \{\theta_i\}_{i \in [1,k]}$.

Note that such a mixture model is quite similar to the two-component mixture model for feedback which we discussed in Section 5.3.1. There, we have just two components, one is fixed to model the background words and the other to model the topic captured by the feedback documents. Indeed, as will be further explained later, the two-component feedback model can be regarded as a two-component PLSA model with an infinitely strong prior to fix some parameters to constants.

To perform latent semantic analysis with PLSA, we would fit the model to our text data and estimate the parameters using either the maximum likelihood (ML) estimator or the maximum a posteriori (MAP) estimator, both can be computed efficiently with the Expectation-Maximization (EM) algorithm. Specifically, with the ML estimator, we would solve the following optimization problem:

$$\Lambda^* = \arg \max_{\Lambda} p(C|\Lambda) \, .$$

The updating formulas of the EM algorithm are:

$$p(z_{D,w} = i) = \frac{p^{(n)}(i|D)p^{(n)}(w\,|\,\theta_i)}{\sum_{i'=1}^{k} p^{(n)}(i'|D)p^{(n)}(w\,|\,\theta_{i'})} \tag{7.1}$$

$$p^{(n+1)}(w\,|\,\theta_i) = \frac{\sum_{D \in C} c(w, D)p(z_{D,w} = i)}{\sum_{w' \in V} \sum_{D \in C} c(w', D)p(z_{D,w'} = i)} \tag{7.2}$$

$$p^{(n+1)}(i\,|\,D) = \frac{\sum_{w \in V} c(w, D)p(z_{D,w} = i)}{\sum_{i'=1}^{k} \sum_{w \in V} c(w, D)p(z_{D,w} = i')} \tag{7.3}$$

where $z_{D,w} \in [1, k]$ is a hidden variable indicating which topic model has been used to generate word w in document D, and the superscripts n and $n + 1$ indicate the iterations. (See Section 5.3.1.1 for an intuitive explanation of such an EM algorithm.)

Given the similarity between PLSA and the two component mixture model discussed in Section 5.3.1, it is not surprising that these EM updating formulas are also very similar to those in Section 5.3.1. A main difference is that we now have far more parameters to estimate, and this does raise a concern, i.e., there will be many local maxima for the likelihood function and the EM algorithm can be easily trapped in a nonoptimal one. This is a general problem with many generative models when the model is complex but the data is relatively sparse.

The solution to this problem generally falls into the following four strategies: (1) Perform multiple trials with different starting points and choose the one that gives the highest likelihood. (2) Modify the algorithm so that it would "explore" the solution space more before committing to a particular local maximum. (3) Regularize the model with prior or a constraint so that the model becomes more rigid and the number of local maxima would be reduced. (4) Use some prior knowledge to determine a good starting point. Strategy (2) is essentially similar to strategy (1) except that in (2), the exploration of different local maxima is not random, but controlled by an additional "annealing" parameter introduced into the EM algorithm. By varying this parameter, we can control the EM algorithm so that it would initially explore more local maxima before it converges to a to a (relatively good) local maximum. A detailed description of such a strategy for estimating PLSA (called tempered EM) can be found in [32]. Strategies (3) and (4) are similar in that both rely on some additional knowledge about the problem to be solved.

Indeed, one advantage of PLSA is that we can naturally incorporate such extra knowledge through defining priors on parameters and using the MAP estimator. Specifically, we would encode our preferences with a prior $p(\Lambda)$, and solve the following optimization problem:

$$\Lambda^* = \arg\max_{\Lambda} p(C|\Lambda)p(\Lambda) .$$

Since Λ consists of parameter about the topic selection probabilities for each document and specific word distributions of the topic models, we can use $p(\Lambda)$ to specify our preferences on what kinds of topics we would like to discover and/or add our knowledge about which document covers which topic(s). For example, if we want to extract topics from reviews of a laptop and are particularly interested in aspects such as battery life, screen size, and memory, we may specify a Dirichlet prior on the topic models to "force" three of the k topic models to assign relatively high probabilities to words such as "battery life," "screen size," and "memory," respectively. Since Dirichlet distribution is a conjugate prior for multinomial distributions, we only need to slightly modify the M-step for re-estimating θ_i in the EM algorithm to incorporate this prior [179].

In general, we may define the following conjugate prior on θ_i:

$$p(\theta_i) \propto \prod_{w \in V} p(w|\theta_i)^{\alpha_w}$$

where α_w is a parameter of the Dirichlet distribution, which can be interpreted as the extra pseudo count of word w to encourage the estimated model θ_i to assign a higher probability to word w. For example, we may want to set the α for words "battery" and "life" both to a number such as 5 and set the α for all other words to zero. This would make θ_i assign relatively higher probability to these two words and other co-occurring words with them.

Using the conjugate prior defined above, we may then compute the MAP estimate by modifying the EM algorithm above to use the following modified M-step to re-estimate θ_i:

$$p^{(n+1)}(w \mid \theta_i) = \frac{\sum_{D \in C} c(w, D) p(z_{D,w} = i) + \alpha_w}{\sum_{w' \in V} (\sum_{D \in C} c(w', D) p(z_{D,w'} = i) + \alpha_w)}.$$

Clearly, if we parameterize α_w based on a reference distribution $p(w|\phi_i)$ such that $\alpha_w = \mu p(w|\phi_i)$, we would essentially favor an estimated θ_i close to ϕ_i. Here μ indicates the strength on the prior and in effect, would balance the pseudo counts from the prior ($\mu p(w|\phi_i)$) and the "collected" counts from the EM algorithm (i.e., $\sum_{D \in C} c(w, D) p(z_{D,w} = i)$). In an extreme case, we can set $\mu = \infty$, which would cause $\theta_i = \phi_i$, i.e., we would set θ_i to a pre-given fixed distribution ϕ_i. Thus, the two-component feedback mixture model discussed in Section 5.3.1 can be regarded as a two-component PLSA model, in which an infinitely strong prior has been placed on one of the components to fix it to the background language model.

Intuitively, the learned topic models capture word clusters based on co-occurrences since if θ_i assigns a high probability to word u, it would tend to be selected frequently in a document where u occurs frequently, and thus it would be encouraged to also assign a high probability to other words in such a document in order to maximize the likelihood. Note that with PLSA, all the words in the collection are generated using the same k latent topic models, but different documents differ in their topic selection distributions.

Since the k topic models used to generate each document are the same, they can be regarded as defining a common k-dimensional semantic space, each dimension being characterized by a word distribution θ_i. A document D's topic selection distribution $\{p(i|D)\}_{i \in [1,k]}$ can thus be regarded as a new representation of D in the k-dimensional semantic space. Since k is typically much smaller than the number of words in the original vocabulary, we are essentially mapping the representation of a document from its original high-dimensional space (i.e., original term space) into a new representation in a low-dimensional latent semantic space. This process is often called *dimension reduction*.

Dimension reduction has traditionally been done through an algebraic approach called Latent Semantic Analysis (LSA) or Latent Semantic Indexing (LSI) [31]. PLSA achieves the same goal with a pure probabilistic approach, which has several advantages: (1) Each semantic dimension is represented with a unigram language model, which is more meaningful than the eigenvector used in LSA to represent a dimension. (2) It is possible to inject domain knowledge into the latent semantic analysis process in PLSA through imposing priors on the parameters of PLSA, but it is harder to do that in LSA. (3) It is possible to add additional latent variables to PLSA to generate more sophisticated latent semantic structures than the flat structure of k latent topics (e.g., a hierarchical structure of topics). These advantages indeed have motivated some follow-up work on extending PLSA, such as automatic labeling of a topic model to help interpret it [180], partitioning a text collection with ad hoc aspects [181], hierarchical PLSA [182], and contextualized PLSA [183].

7.2   LATENT DIRICHLET ALLOCATION (LDA)

Although PLSA has been shown to be effective in many applications, it has two deficiencies: First, it is not really a generative model because the topic selection probability is defined in a document-specific way. That is, $p(i|D)$ is defined based on a specific document D. Thus, the learned values of $p(i|D)$ cannot be used to generate a new document which is different from D. Second, PLSA has many parameters, making it hard to find a global maximum in parameter estimation as we discussed earlier.

To address these limitations, Blei et al. [172] proposed Latent Dirichlet Allocation (LDA) as an extension of PLSA. The main idea is to define $p(i|D)$ in a "generative" way by drawing the distribution $p(i|D)$ from a Dirichlet distribution when generating a document. Once we draw $p(i|D)$, we then use this to generate all the words in D. This not only gives us a generative model that can be used to sample "future documents," but also reduces the number of parameters significantly.

Formally, the probability of generating a document D of length $|D|$ is now:

$$p(D|\Lambda) = \int_{\Delta} Dir(\pi|\alpha_1, ..., \alpha_k) \prod_{j=1}^{|D|} (\sum_{i=1}^{k} p(w_j|\theta_i) p(i|\pi)) d\pi$$

where $D = w_1...w_{|D|}$, and Δ is the $k-1$-dimensional simplex containing all the possible values for π. $\Lambda = \{\alpha_1, ..., \alpha_k, \theta_1, ..., \theta_k\}$ is the set of all parameters; each θ_i is a multinomial distribution over words as in the case of PLSA. $\alpha_1, ..., \alpha_k$ are the parameters of the Dirichlet distribution $Dir(\pi|\alpha_1, ..., \alpha_k)$.

We may understand this likelihood function by imagining the following process of generating a document of length $|D|$. First, we would choose a topic selection distribution π by sampling from the Dirichlet distribution $Dir(\pi|\alpha_1, ..., \alpha_k)$. The obtained π is a multinomial distribution over all the k topics, and it essentially determines the topic coverage in the document to be generated in the sense that if π gives a topic, say θ_1, a very high probability, then θ_1 would be used very often to generate a word in the document. Second, we would generate a word by first sampling a topic θ_i using $p(i|\pi)$ and then sampling a word from $p(w|\theta_i)$. We repeat this second step $|D|$ times to generate all the words in this document.

Clearly, the second step is essentially the same as in PLSA, but the first step changes the model in two important ways: (1) $p(i|\pi)$ is no longer dependent on the specific document to be generated, making LDA a generative model that can be used to generate a new document. (2) There is now only one set of k parameters $\{\alpha_i, ..., \alpha_k\}$ for all the documents to *indirectly* control the topic coverages in all the documents as opposed to $k|C|$ parameters in PLSA to allow each document to have its own independent topic coverage distribution $p(i|D)$. Having fewer parameters means that the problem of multiple local maxima is less severe than in PLSA. To further reduce the number of parameters, we can also let each θ_i be drawn from another Dirichlet distribution; see [172] for more discussion about this variation.

As in the case of PLSA, we can also fit LDA to a collection of documents and use the maximum likelihood estimator to estimate the parameters Λ (called empirical Bayes [184]):

$$\Lambda^* = \arg\max_{\Lambda} \prod_{D \in C} p(D|\Lambda)$$

where C is a collection of documents.

However, unlike the ML estimate of PLSA which can be easily computed using the EM algorithm, the ML estimate of the LDA model is much harder to compute due to the more complex form of the likelihood function. For the same reason, inferences such as to compute $p(\pi|D, \Lambda)$ are also hard to compute. Thus, an approximation method is usually used for parameter estimation and inferences with LDA.

A convexity-based variational approximation of LDA was proposed by Blei and co-authors when they introduced LDA in [172]. The main idea is to use Jensen's inequality to define a lower-bound function for the log-likelihood function. The lower-bound function is parameterized by a set of variational parameters which can control the tightness of the bound. The overall procedure for parameter estimation is an iterative algorithm similar to EM, in which we would iteratively optimize the lower-bound (making it as close to the likelihood function as possible) and then re-estimate parameters by maximizing the lower-bound of the likelihood function. Such a variational EM algorithm is essentially the same as the EM algorithm for estimating a PLSA model except that the E-step is not to compute the expectation of the complete likelihood, but to optimize the lower-bound through varying the variational parameters. Another difference is that now neither the E-step nor the M-step can be carried out analytically, so numerical optimization has to be done [172].

Specifically, in the variational E-step, our goal is to compute two sets of variational parameters for each document D based on the current generation of parameter values obtained in the EM algorithm: (1) $\{\gamma_{D,i}\}_{i=1}^{k}$: Dirichlet parameters for approximating the posterior distribution of π. That is, we assume that the posterior distribution of π given document D is the Dirichlet distribution $Dir(\gamma_{D,1}, ..., \gamma_{D,k})$. (2) $\{p(z_{D,w} = i)\}$: Multinomial parameters for approximating the posterior distribution of a set of hidden variables $\{z_{D,w} \in [1, k]\}$ that indicate which topic (θ_i) has been used to generate word w in document D. These hidden variables are essentially the same as in the PLSA estimation discussed earlier[1], and we also have $\sum_{i=1}^{k} p(z_{D,w} = i) = 1$.

The variational parameters are computed by iteratively updating them with the following formulas with an initial value such as $p^{(0)}(z_{D,w} = i) = 1/k$:

$$
p^{(t+1)}(z_{D,w} = i) \quad \propto \quad p^{(n)}(w|\theta_i) exp\left(\Phi(\gamma_{D,i}^{(t)}) - \Phi(\sum_{j=1}^{k} \gamma_{D,j})\right)
$$

$$
\gamma_{D,i}^{(t)} \quad = \quad \alpha_i + \sum_{w \in V} c(w, D) p^{(t)}(z_{D,w} = i)
$$

where Φ is the first derivative of the log Γ function which can be computed using Taylor approximation [172]. The iterative updating is repeated until convergence.

Comparing this variational E-step with the E-step in the EM algorithm for PLSA, we see that we are computing similar values with the following difference: Unlike $p(i|D)$, which is computed independently for each document D, $\gamma_{D,i}$ depends on the global parameter values α_i. Intuitively, this is the consequence of imposing of a Dirichlet distribution in LDA to regularize $p(i|D)$. $\gamma_{D,i}$ customizes γ_i for document D based on how many words in D are believed to be generated from topic θ_i (captured by the second term in the updating formula).

In the M-step, we then use the computed $\{\gamma_{D,i}, p(z_{D,w} = i)_i\}_{i=1}^{k}$ for each document D to re-estimate α_i and $p(w|\theta_i)$. The updating formula for $p(w|\theta_i)$ can be analytically obtained as:

$$
p^{(n+1)}(w|\theta_i) \propto \sum_{D \in C} c(w, D) p(z_{D,w} = i)
$$

which again is the same as in PLSA. However, the re-estimation formula of α_i cannot be obtained analytically because the derivative equation does not have an analytical solution. In [172], a linear time Newton-Ralphson algorithm is used to iteratively update α_i based on $\{\gamma_{D,i}\}_{D \in C, i \in [1,k]}$ and the value of α_i from the previous iteration.

The inference of parameters like π for a (possibly new) document can be done by doing one E-step based on known α_i and $p(w|\theta_i)$ rather than their tentative values as in the EM algorithm.

Other approximation algorithms, such as expectation propagation [185] and Markov chain Monte Carlo [186, 187], have also been proposed to solve the problem of estimation and inferences with LDA.

7.3   EXTENSIONS OF PLSA AND LDA

PLSA and LDA represent two basic formulations of topic language models. Since they were proposed, many extensions of them have been made. In [188], PLSA is combined with a hidden Markov

---

[1]In [172], a different notation is used for $p(z_{D,w} = i)$ (i.e., ϕ_{ni}). Here we use $p(z_{D,w} = i)$ to be consistent with the notation we used for PLSA.

model (HMM) to obtain an Aspect HMM (AHMM), which can be used to segment text based on topic transitions. In [182], PLSA is extended to model a topic hierarchy so that topic models with different granularity levels can be learned from text data in an unsupervised manner. The idea is to define a topic tree to represent the multiple levels of abstraction of topics so that the leaf topics would characterize very specialized topics unique to a few documents, while the root topic would capture the general topic in the entire set of documents. The PLSA model can then be extended to generate a document in the following way. First, we choose a leaf node from the tree, which would uniquely determine a path from the root to this leaf node. This choice is made once for a document. We would then use the standard PLSA to generate all the words in the document by restricting the choices of topics to the topics corresponding to the nodes in the chosen path. Thus, depending on the choice of the path (equivalently the leaf node), a potentially different set of topics would be mixed to generate a different document. The model can be estimated using the EM algorithm in mostly the same way as in the case of the standard PLSA. This model can also be regarded as an extension of the distributional clustering model [189, 190], which differs from PLSA in that all the words in a document are assumed to be generated using the *same* word distribution, though there are multiple candidate distributions to be used; in PLSA, different words in the same document can be generated using potentially a *different* word distribution.

In [191], a background topic is introduced to PLSA to make the extracted topic models more focusing on the content words rather than the common words in the collection. In the same work, PLSA is also extended to model multiple collections of documents with component topic models tied across collections. Such a cross-collection mixture model can be used to extract common topics covered in all the collections of documents as well as the corresponding variations of a topic in each collection. A more general way to incorporate context variables into PLSA is presented in [183], and a new model called Contextual Probabilistic Latent Semantic Analysis (CPLSA) is proposed.

In CPLSA, a document is assumed to be associated with *contexts*. A context can be the time, location, source, or other meta data associated with a document. In general, it defines a partition of a set of documents. For example, the time context would group documents with the same time stamp together. Multiple contexts can have overlapping partitions. The main extension of PLSA made in CPLSA is to introduce: (1) multiple versions of the word distributions for topics (called *multiple views* of topics) corresponding to different contexts (e.g., multiple time points); and (2) multiple versions of the topic coverage distribution for each document again corresponding to different contexts. Thus, the component models to be actually mixed when generating words in each document can vary according to the context(s) of the document. As a result, we may discover topic variations according to context (context-specific views of topics) and reveal potentially different topic coverages in different contexts. By instantiating the general CPLSA with different contexts, we may obtain many specific models suitable for a variety of contextual text mining tasks, such as comparative analysis of documents about similar topics [191], spatiotemporal topic pattern mining [183], author-topic analysis [192], and event impact analysis [183]. PLSA has also been extended to incorporate two special word distributions to capture positive and negative sentiment in text [193]. Such a topic sentiment mixture model can be regarded as a special case of CPLSA with sentiment corresponding to "implicit context," and has been shown to be able to generate interesting tabular opinion summaries for a set of documents. In [205], PLSA is extended to model coordinated multiple text streams (e.g., news articles in multiple languages such as English and Chinese) and discover correlated bursty topic patterns. This extension can also be regarded as an instantiation of the general CPLSA with each stream as a different context.

Another recent extension of PLSA is to extend it to analyze a text collection with network structures [194]. The basic idea is to use the network structure associated with text documents to impose soft constraints on parameters of a topic model like PLSA. For example, a constraint may say that the topic coverages of two documents that are connected in the network should be similar. Conceptually, imposing such constraints is similar to adding a prior on the model parameters, and this is achieved here by defining penalty terms using a network structure and adding them to the likelihood function of PLSA (the new model is called NetPLSA). Such a model can combine social network analysis with topic modeling of text. The added network structure is shown to help improve topic modeling results [194].

LDA has also been extended in many ways. In [195], LDA is extended to learn a topic hierarchy, which is similar to the extension of PLSA in [182] to learn a topic hierarchy with the main difference being that the tree is not fixed in advance; instead, the tree is being generated using a nested Chinese Restaurant Process (CRP) [195]. The levels of the tree still need to be fixed in advance, but the number of topics at each level can be potentially infinite. Thus, there are potentially an infinite number of paths of any given length. The nested CRP essentially defines a distribution over all these possible paths. When we generate a document, we would first sample a path according to this distribution. After that, the rest of the generation process is the same as in the standard LDA but the choices of topics are restricted to those in the path chosen.

In [196], an extension of LDA (called correspondence LDA) is proposed to model annotated data (e.g., images with captions). The basic idea is to have a generative model for image regions (Gaussian) and another generative model for the caption text (multinomial). Two corresponding mixture models can then be defined to model regions and captions with a set of common latent (semantic) factors; the multinomial distribution of the latent factors is drawn from a Dirichlet distribution as in the standard LDA. The key idea of the correspondence LDA is to coordinate the drawing of the latent factor distribution so that an image and its caption would share the same latent factor distribution. Moreover, after choosing some latent factors to generate all the regions in an image, only those *chosen* latent factors would be allowed to be used to generate the words in the caption. Note that if we remove this constraint, the generation of words and image regions would not be so much coordinated even though they all would sample latent factors using the same latent factor distribution. In an extreme case, they may chose two disjoint sets of factors.

The choices of a topic for generating adjacent words in a document are made independently in the standard LDA. To capture the syntax of text, LDA has been extended in [197] to introduce dependency between the topics used to generate adjacent words through a hidden Markov model

(HMM). A state of the HMM indicates a class of topics. A special state is used to denote a mixture of semantic topics, and when we generate a word from this state, the process would be the same as the standard LDA (i.e., one topic from a set of semantic topics would be chosen first and then a word would be drawn according to the word distribution of the chosen topic). All other states are syntactic states. Each syntactic state has just one word distribution for outputing words, thus when we generate a word from such a state, we would not need to pick a topic from a set of topics as in the case of the special semantic state mentioned above. By fitting such a model to text, we can learn word distributions corresponding to various syntactic classes through the syntactic states of HMM, while at the same time we also learn various subtopics through the special semantic topic state.

In order to model topic evolution over time, a dynamic topic model is proposed in [198]. This model can be regarded as an adaptation of LDA to model a stream of text documents with time slices. If we use the standard LDA on such data, we may fit a separate LDA to the documents in each time slice. But the models estimated in this way would be independent of each other. A key idea of the dynamic topic model is to model the evolution of parameters of LDA (i.e., Dirichlet parameters $\{\alpha_i\}$ and multinomial parameters $\{p(w|\theta_i)\}$) over time with a state space model that evolves with Gaussian noise. That is, the parameters at time $t + 1$ are assumed to follow a Gaussian distribution with the mean being the corresponding parameters at time t and some constant variances. The model is shown to work well on a set of 30,000 articles from *Science* spanning 120 years from 1881 through 2000, revealing interesting evolution patterns of topics [198].

The author-topic model [192, 199] extends LDA by including the authorship information. The main difference from LDA is as follows. Each author is associated with a distribution over the topics (i.e., topic coverage) which is drawn from a Dirichlet distribution. When we generate a word in a document, we would first choose one of the authors of the document, and use the associated distribution to further choose a topic and generate the word. If each document is written by precisely one author and no author has written more than one document, then the model recovers LDA. Several interesting applications of this model are presented in [192].

Another interesting extension of LDA is the correlated topic models presented in [200]. In the standard LDA, the coverage of topics is determined by a multinomial distribution drawn from a Dirichlet distribution. Thus, it does not capture the potential dependency between different but related topics. In the correlated topic model, this limitation is removed by replacing the Dirichlet distribution with a logistic normal distribution which can potentially capture the dependency among topics through the covariance matrix. Note that hierarchical topic models also capture the dependency among topics, but they tend to impose a rigid dependency structure. The correlated topic model is more flexible and can capture the underlying natural correlations between topics. Another extension of LDA with a similar motivation is the Pachinko Allocation Machine (PAM) introduced in [201]. While the correlated topic model captures only pair-wise correlations of topics, PAM can potentially capture arbitrary-arity, nested topic correlations.

7.4   TOPIC MODEL LABELING

A fundamental assumption made in all these topic models is that a topic can be represented by a multinomial distribution. When such models are used for text mining, we would face the question of how to interpret a multinomial word distribution. Intuitively, the high probability words of a topic model often suggest some coherent topic, but it would be desirable to label a topic with more informative phrases. In [180], several probabilistic approaches are proposed to automatically label a topic model. The general procedure consists of the following steps:

First, a set of candidate phrases are generated either by parsing the text collection or using statistical measures such as mutual information. Second, these candidate phrases are ranked based on a probabilistic measure, which indicates how well a phrase can characterize a topic model. Finally, a few top-ranked phrases would be chosen as labels of a topic model. The selected labels can be diversified through eliminating redundancy.

In [180], two measures are proposed to rank phrases. In the first, we simply rank a phrase based on the likelihood of the phrase given the topic model. Intuitively this would give us meaningful phrases with high probabilities according to the word distribution of the topic model to be labeled. In the second, we rank a phrase based on the expectation of the mutual information between a word and the phrase taken under the word distribution of the topic model. This second method is shown to be better than the first because it would favor a phrase that has an *overall* similarity to the high probability words of the topic model. Furthermore, a topic can also be labeled with respect to an arbitrary reference/context collection to enable an interpretation of the topic in different contexts [180].

7.5   USING TOPIC MODELS FOR RETRIEVAL

An immediate application of topic models for information retrieval is to represent text in a low-dimensional semantic space. In traditional retrieval models, a document and a query are generally represented as a "bag of words," and matching a query with a document is also performed at the level of words. This has two potential deficiencies:

First, words as semantic dimensions are not orthogonal. Indeed, in a bag-of-words representation, redundancy and dependency between words are not captured, thus matching two related words such as "president" and "government" would be counted as independent evidence toward scoring. Second, synonyms are not matched with each other; thus only an exact matching of words can contribute to scoring. For example, "car" in a query would not match with "vehicle" in a document.

A natural solution to overcome these deficiencies is to represent a document at the level of *semantic concepts*. A semantic concept can be roughly understood as a cluster of words that are semantically related to each other (e.g., "car," "drive," and "vehicle"). As discussed earlier in Section 7.1, topic models provide a good way to achieve this goal. Specifically, each topic model (word distribution) can represent a latent semantic concept, and the topic coverage distribution $p(i|D)$ in PLSA (or π in LDA) can serve as a new representation of document D in the low-dimensional semantic space.

We can thus map a query and a document both to this semantic space and match them accordingly. This idea has been explored in [32] and [106]. Since co-occurring words are now "grouped" into the same topic model (i.e., they are assigned high probabilities by the same topic model), the latent semantic dimensions defined in this way are more orthogonal than those based on individual words. Also, semantically related words can now match each other indirectly through "belonging to" the same word distribution characterizing a topic. Thus, the two deficiencies mentioned above can both be addressed.

However, matching documents with queries using *solely* their representations in such a low-dimensional space has also its own deficiency: we can no longer easily distinguish the finer granularity difference in the meanings of those semantically related words, i.e., there is a lack of discrimination. This is especially true if the number of semantic dimensions is not sufficiently high. Indeed, when we map a document from the original word-based representation into the semantic topic-based representation, we have lost information about the original words. For example, while we know that the document covers a topic aspect corresponding to "government," we would not know which aspect(s) of "government" it covers (e.g., "president" vs. "congress"). Because of this reason, matching solely on latent semantic representation can only be expected to increase recall (i.e., help retrieving more relevant documents) but likely would hurt the precision in top-ranked documents. Indeed, in both [32] and [106], it was found to be most effective if we combine such a low-dimensional semantic representation with the original high-dimensional space representation based on words (e.g., combining the scores of a document using both representations). Intuitively, such a combination allows us to both benefit from the latent semantic representation in matching semantically related words and retain the needed discrimination from the word-level representation.

Another application of topic models for retrieval is for smoothing. Specifically, once we learn a set of unigram language models characterizing the latent topics, $\{p(w|\theta_i)\}_{i=1}^{k}$, we can compute the following predictive distribution given a document D:

$$p_{topic}(w|D) = \sum_{i=1}^{k} p(\theta_i|D)p(w|\theta_i)$$

and then use this distribution as our document language model for retrieval. That is, we may assume $p(w|\theta_D) = p_{topic}(w|D)$ and use either the query likelihood retrieval model or the KL-divergence retrieval model to score documents.

Since $p(w|\theta_i)$ is learned from a collection of documents, it would likely give many words not occurring in document D a nonzero probability. This is why $p_{topic}(w|D)$ can achieve the purpose of smoothing. Indeed, words that are semantically related to (co-occurring with) words in D would tend to have relatively high probabilities. Intuitively, we may imagine each θ_i represents a cluster of documents. Thus, $p(\theta_i|D)$ indicates which cluster more likely contains D, and the equation above is simply a weighted combination of all the unigram language models corresponding to these clusters.

In [118], retrieval with such a smoothing method using topics learned from an LDA model is studied. In this work, $p_{topic}(w|D)$ is further interpolated with the maximum likelihood estimate of the document model $p_{ml}(w|\theta_D)$ and the collection language model. As discussed above, the interpolation with the maximum likelihood estimate is desirable; it helps achieve the discrimination power based on the original word representation. The interpolation with the collection language model is also essential to achieve an IDF effect (see Section 3.4). The results of LDA model are shown to be better than the regular cluster-based smoothing methods proposed in [107], but they are worse than the results of the relevance model, which may indicate that global co-occurrences in the whole collection are not as useful as local co-occurrences in the top ranked documents. However, a combination of the LDA model with the relevance model is shown to outperform the relevance model, suggesting that the LDA model and relevance model capture different kinds of co-occurrences, and they can be combined to benefit from both kinds of co-occurrences.

Yet another important application of topic models to improve a retrieval system is to use them to extract topics and summarize/organize search results. Indeed, the basic topic models such as PLSA and LDA can already be used to organize search results based on topics.

In [181], an extension of the standard PLSA is proposed to allow a user to flexibly specify the aspects to be used for generating an overview of a set of documents. This method would allow a user to iteratively refine and organize search results based on meaningful ad hoc aspects described with keywords. The tabular aspect sentiment summary generated using techniques described in [193] can be very useful for summarizing opinions in search results.

In general, topic models have been shown to be very useful for mining topics and analyzing topic patterns in text. They can potentially extend a search engine to go beyond search to generate knowledge.

7.6   SUMMARY

In this chapter, we reviewed a family of language models that all attempt to model the latent topics in text. They can all be useful for discovering and analyzing latent topics in text. We have provided a relatively detailed description of the two basic representative models, i.e., PLSA and LDA, and summarized a number of extensions made to both of them.

We further discussed how to label a topic model to help interpret a topic model in an application context, and presented three uses of topic models for information retrieval: (1) representing text in low-dimensional semantic space; (2) smoothing document language models; and (3) summarizing and organizing search results. Promising results have been reported in all these directions.

It is worth pointing out that as two basic topic models, PLSA and LDA have not been systematically compared for improving a retrieval system. As a generative model, LDA is advantageous over PLSA, but for the purpose of obtaining a low dimension representation of text and extraction of topics, it is unclear whether LDA is necessarily better than PLSA especially when we have extra knowledge that can be leveraged to impose priors on PLSA parameters. Intuitively, regularizing the topic choices with a parametric Dirichlet distribution may cause the estimated topic coverage distribution in LDA to be less discriminative than the corresponding distribution in PLSA. A systematic comparison of PLSA and LDA for information retrieval would be needed in order to understand the influence of their difference in modeling on the performance of a retrieval task.

CHAPTER 8

Conclusions

As an essential tool to help people combat information overload, search engines have become more and more important in our lives. The accuracy of a search engine is mostly determined by its underlying retrieval model. Thus, seeking an optimal retrieval model has been a long-standing central problem in information retrieval research. In this book, we have systematically reviewed a family of new probabilistic information retrieval models based on statistical language modeling with an emphasis on the underlying principles, empirically effective language models, and language models developed for nontraditional retrieval tasks. In this last chapter, we highlight some of the most important points made in the previous chapters, provide a big picture of the work surveyed, and offer an outlook for the future of this research area.

8.1 LANGUAGE MODELS VS. TRADITIONAL RETRIEVAL MODELS

It has been a long-standing challenge in IR research to develop robust and effective retrieval models. As a new generation of probabilistic retrieval models, language modeling approaches have several advantages over traditional retrieval models, especially the vector-space model:

First, language modeling approaches generally have a good statistical foundation, which offers two important benefits: (1) It enables us to leverage many established statistical estimation methods to set parameters in a retrieval function. For example, using a fairly standard Bayesian estimation method, we could easily derive Dirichlet prior smoothing, which is now one of the most effective smoothing methods (see Section 3.3.3). Also, the EM algorithm has been quite useful for estimating models such as the mixture feedback model (see Section 5.3.1). (2) It helps clarify what assumptions about data modeling are made in a retrieval function, and a good understanding of such assumptions helps diagnose the weakness and strength of a model and better interpret experiment results. For example, the two-stage language model has allowed us to better explain why the sensitivity curves of a smoothing parameter vary according to the queries, and to further improve our estimate of smoothing parameters (see Section 3.5).

Note that while the vector space model clearly lacks a statistical foundation, it would be unfair to say that the classical probabilistic retrieval models [56, 57, 58] lack a statistical foundation. Quite the opposite: they are solid probabilistic models and we might call them language models as well. Indeed, theoretically speaking, any retrieval model that relies on a probabilistic model of text can be called a language modeling approach, thus the term "language modeling approach" or "language model" alone does not really differentiate these new models from a traditional probabilistic model. The real difference between them seems to lie in how we handle the parameters of a probabilistic model. In the studies of the traditional probabilistic models, less emphasis has been placed on how to improve the estimate of the parameters, which has turned out to be quite important as shown in virtually all the recent work on using language models for retrieval. As a result, although those traditional probabilistic models are theoretically sound, they tend to not perform well without heuristic modifications of the formula. In contrast, in the new language modeling approaches, much emphasis has been put on applying solid statistical estimation methods (e.g., maximum likelihood estimator, maximum a posteriori estimator, and EM algorithm). Recent work has also put more emphasis on using multinomial distributions to model text, which naturally capture term frequencies. For example, the relevance model (see Section 5.3.3) essentially provides a good way to estimate the parameters in a traditional document-generation probabilistic model (see Section 2.2) when we do not have relevance judgments.

Second, language models provide a principled way to address the critical issue of text representation and term weighting. The issue of term weighting has long been recognized as critical, but before language modeling approaches were proposed, this issue had been traditionally addressed mostly in a heuristic way. Language models, multinomial unigram language models particular, can incorporate term frequencies and document length normalization naturally into a probabilistic model. While such connection has also been made in a classical probabilistic retrieval model (e.g., [56]), the estimation of parameters was not addressed as seriously as in the language models.

Third, language models can often be more easily adapted to model various kinds of complex and special retrieval problems than traditional models as we discussed in Chapter 6. This benefit has largely come from the availability of many well-understood statistical models such as finite mixture models which can be estimated efficiently using the EM algorithm. Indeed, the benefit goes beyond search to discovering and analyzing latent topics in text as we discussed in Chapter 7.

However, the language modeling approaches also have some deficiencies as compared with traditional models:

First, there is a lack of *explicit* discrimination in most of the language models developed so far. For example, in the query likelihood retrieval function, the IDF effect is achieved through smoothing the document language model with a background model. While this can be explained by modeling the noise in the query, it seems to be a rather unnatural way to penalize matching common words, at least as compared with the traditional TF-IDF weighting. Such a lack of discrimination is indeed a general problem with all generative models as they are designed to describe what the data looks like rather than how the data differs. This weakness indicates that there is still some gap between the current language models and what we need to accurately model relevance, and there is room for further improving the current models. Indeed, constraint analysis in [28] has shown that the query likelihood retrieval function does not satisfy all the desirable constraints unconditionally.

Second, the language models have been found to be less robust than the traditional TF-IDF model in some cases and can perform poorly or be very sensitive to parameter setting. For example, the feedback methods proposed in [134] are shown to be sensitive to parameter setting, whereas a traditional method such as Rocchio appears to be more robust. This may be the reason why language models have not yet been able to outperform well-tuned, full-fledged traditional methods consistently and convincingly. In particular, BM25 term weighting coupled with Rocchio feedback (see Chapter 2) remains a strong baseline which is at least as competitive as any language modeling approach for many tasks.

Third, some sophisticated language models can be computationally expensive (e.g., the translation model), which may limit their uses in large-scale retrieval applications. Also, many sophisticated topic models discussed in Chapter 7 are also very complex to estimate, making it infeasible to run them on a dynamic result set of documents in online retrieval systems.

Thus, although the language modeling approaches are quite promising and have a great potential to further develop, whether they will eventually replace the traditional retrieval models remains an interesting open question.

8.2   SUMMARY OF RESEARCH PROGRESS

Since the pioneering work by Ponte and Croft [74], a lot of progress has been made in studying the language modeling approaches to IR. Here we attempt to highlight some of the most important developments:

- Framework and justification for using LMs for IR: the query likelihood retrieval method has been shown to be a well-justified model according to the probability ranking principle [55]. General frameworks such as the risk minimization framework [1, 89, 90] and the generative relevance framework [92] offer road maps for systematically applying language models to retrieval problems.

- Many effective models have been developed and they often work well for multiple tasks:

  - The KL-divergence retrieval model [1, 134, 92], which covers query likelihood retrieval model as a special case, has been found to be a solid and empirically effective retrieval model. It can flexibly incorporate different estimation methods to improve the estimate of document language models and query language models.

  - Dirichlet prior smoothing has been recognized as an effective smoothing method for retrieval [94]. The KL-divergence retrieval model combined with Dirichlet prior smoothing represents the current state of the art baseline method (without pseudo feedback) for the language modeling approaches to IR.

  - The translation model proposed in [110] is an elegant and powerful extension of the simple query likelihood retrieval model. It enables handling polysemy and synonyms in a principled way with a great potential for supporting semantic information retrieval. It naturally supports cross-lingual information retrieval and has been shown to perform very well.

  - Relevance model [71, 92] offers an elegant solution to the estimation problem in the classical probabilistic retrieval model as well as serves as an effective feedback method for the KL-divergence retrieval model. It has been successfully applied to many different retrieval tasks with good performance.

- – Mixture unigram language models have been shown to be very powerful and can be useful for many purposes such as pseudo feedback [134], improving model discriminativeness [125], and modeling redundancy [176, 91].

- It has been shown that completely automatic tuning of parameters is possible for both non-feedback retrieval [109] and pseudo feedback [139].

- LMs can be applied to virtually any retrieval task with great potential for modeling complex IR problems (as surveyed in Chapter 6).

- Probabilistic topic models are quite powerful for discovering and analyzing topic patterns in text. The two basic representative models are the probabilistic latent semantic analysis model (PLSA) [32, 178] and the latent Dirichlet allocation model (LDA) [172]. These topic models can be applied to improve the utility of a retrieval system through offering a low-dimensional semantic representation of text, smoothing of language models, and summarizing search results.

For practitioners who want to apply language models to specific applications, the KL-divergence retrieval function combined with Dirichlet prior smoothing for estimating document language models and either relevance model or mixture model for estimating query language models can be highly recommended. Such a configuration has performed well in many studies and often outperforms other configurations of models. All the models involved in such a configuration have been implemented in the Lemur retrieval toolkit available at `http://www.lemurproject.org/`. This toolkit is designed to be extensible for adding new retrieval methods, so it is also relatively easy to adapt or extend the existing models for new tasks. A main deficiency of Lemur is that it currently cannot handle well a very large data set (e.g., more than 500 GB text). While there are some other retrieval toolkits available that can handle much larger data sets, none of the others seems to support language models well. It is thus highly desirable to develop a more scalable retrieval toolkit than Lemur that can support many language models for information retrieval.

8.3   FUTURE DIRECTIONS

Despite much progress has been made in applying language models to IR, there are still many challenges to be solved to fully develop the potential of such models. The following is a list of some interesting opportunities for future research.

Challenge 1: Develop an efficient, robust, and effective language model for ad hoc retrieval that can (1) optimize retrieval parameters automatically, (2) perform as well as or better than well-tuned traditional retrieval methods with pseudo feedback (e.g., BM25 with Rocchio), and (3) be computed as efficiently as traditional retrieval methods. Would some kind of language model eventually replace the currently popular BM25 and Rocchio? How to implement IDF more explicitly in a language modeling approach may be an important issue to further study; axiomatic analysis may be helpful. Relaxing the assumption that the same words occur independently in a document (e.g., by using the Dirichlet Compound Model [202]) may also be necessary to capture TF normalization more accurately.

Challenge 2: Demonstrate consistent and substantial improvement by going beyond unigram language models. While there has been some effort in this direction, the empirical performance improvement of the more sophisticated models over the simple models tends to be insignificant. This is consistent with what has been observed in traditional retrieval models. Would we ever be able to achieve significant improvement over the unigram language models by using higher-order n-gram models or capturing limited syntactic/semantic dependencies among words? As we go beyond unigram language models, reliable estimation of the model becomes more challenging due to the problem of data sparseness. Thus, developing better estimation techniques (e.g., those that can lead to optimal weighting of phrases conditioned on weighting of single words) may be critical for making more progress in this direction.

Challenge 3: Develop language models to support personalized search. Using more user information and a user's search context to better infer a user's information need is essential for optimizing search accuracy. This is especially important when the search results are not satisfactory and the user would reformulate the query many times. How can we use language models to accurately represent a user's interest and further incorporate such knowledge into a retrieval model? Detailed analysis of user actions (e.g., skipping some results and viewing others, deleting query terms but adding them back later, recurring interests vs. ad hoc information needs) may be necessary to obtain an accurate representation of a user's information need.

Challenge 4: Develop language models that can support "life-time learning." One important advantage of language models is the potential benefit from improved estimation of the models based on additional training data. As a search engine is being used, we will be able to collect a lot of implicit feedback information such as clickthroughs. How can we develop language models that can learn from all such feedback information from all the users to optimize retrieval results for future queries? From the viewpoint of personalized search, how can we leverage many users of a system to improve performance for a particular user (i.e., supporting collaborative search)? Translation models appear to be especially promising in this direction, and they are complementary with the recently developed discriminative models for learning to rank documents such as RankNet [203] and Ranking SVM [204]. It should be extremely interesting to study how to combine these two complementary approaches.

Challenge 5: Develop language models that can model document structures and subtopics. Most existing work on studying retrieval models, including work on language models, has assumed a simple bag-of-words representation of text. While such a representation ensures that the model would work for any text, in a specific application, documents often have certain structures that can be potentially exploited to improve search accuracy. For example, often it is some part of a long document that is relevant. How can we model potentially different subtopics in a single document and match only the relevant part of a document with a query? Mixture models and hidden Markov models may be promising in this direction.

Challenge 6: Generalize language models to support ranking of both unstructured and structured data. Traditionally, structured data and unstructured data (text) have been managed in different ways with structured data mainly handled through a relational database while unstructured data through an information retrieval system, leading to two different research communities (i.e., the database community and the information retrieval community). Recently, however, the boundary between the two communities seems to become vague. First, as exploratory search on databases becomes more and more popular on the Web, database researchers are now paying much attention to the problem of ranking structured data in a database. The information needs to be satisfied are very similar to those in a retrieval system. Second, some database fields may contain long text (e.g., abstracts of research papers), while most text documents also have some structured meta-data (e.g., authors, dates). Thus, a very interesting question is whether we can generalize language models to develop unified probabilistic models for searching/ranking both structured data and unstructured data. The INEX initiative (`http://inex.is.informatik.uni-duisburg.de/`) has stimulated a lot of research in developing XML retrieval models (i.e., semi-structured data retrieval models), but we are still far from a unified model for unstructured, semi-structured, and structured data.

Challenge 7: Develop language models for hypertext retrieval. As an abstract representation, the Web can be regarded a hypertext collection. Language models developed so far have not explicitly incorporated hyperlinks and the associated anchor text into the model. How can we use language modeling to develop a hypertext retrieval model for Web search? How should we define a generative model for hypertext?

Challenge 8: Develop/extend language models for retrieval with complex information needs. Language models are natural for modeling topical relevance. But in many retrieval applications, a user's information need consists of multiple dimensions of preferences with topical relevance being only one of them. Other factors such as readability, genre, and sentiment may also be important. How can we use language models to capture such nontopical aspects? How can we develop or extend language models to optimize ranking of documents based on multiple factors? In this direction, recent work has shown that the learning-to-rank approaches are quite promising, thus again it would be very interesting to study how to combine the language modeling approaches (generative approaches) with the learning-to-rank approaches (discriminative approaches).

Challenge 9: Develop efficient algorithms for computing complex language models such as probabilistic topic models. Topic models such as PLSA and LDA have proven very useful for discovering and analyzing topics in text. However, the current algorithms for estimating these models and for making inferences with these models are still time-consuming (especially in the case of LDA), which limits their uses in a real-time online retrieval system. Thus, developing efficient and more scalable algorithms for these models is a highly important research direction.

Bibliography

[1] John Lafferty and ChengXiang Zhai. Document language models, query models, and risk minimization for information retrieval. In *Proceedings of SIGIR'01*, pp. 111–119, Sept. 2001. DOI: 10.1145/383952.383970

[2] Tao Tao, Xuanhui Wang, Qiaozhu Mei, and ChengXiang Zhai. Language model information retrieval with document expansion. In *Proceedings of the main conference on Human Language Technology Conference of the North American Chapter of the Association of Computational Linguistics*, pp. 407–414, Morristown, NJ, 2006. Association for Computational Linguistics. DOI: 10.3115/1220835.1220887

[3] K. Sparck Jones and P. Willett, editors. *Readings in Information Retrieval*. Morgan Kaufmann Publishers, 1997.

[4] Christian Middleton and Ricardo Baeza-Yates. A comparison of open source search engines. http://wrg.upf.edu/WRG/dctos/Middleton-Baeza.pdf.

[5] C. W. Cleverdon, J. Mills, and E. M. Keen. Factors determining the performance of indexing systems, 1966. Cranfield, UK: Aslib Cranfield Research Project, College of Aeronautics (Volume 1:Design; Volume 2: Results).

[6] K. Sparck Jones and K. van Rijsbergen. Report on the need for and provision of an 'ideal' information retrieval test collection, 1975. British Library Research and Development Report 5266, University Computer Laboratory, Cambridge.

[7] Chris Buckley, Darrin Dimmick, Ian Soboroff, and Ellen M. Voorhees. Bias and the limits of pooling for large collections. *Information Retrieval*, 10(6):491–508, 2007. DOI: 10.1007/s10791-007-9032-x

[8] Kalervo Järvelin and Jaana Kekäläinen. Cumulated gain-based evaluation of IR techniques. *ACM Transactions on Information Systems*, 20(4):422–446, 2002. DOI: 10.1145/582415.582418

[9] Diane Kelly and Jaime Teevan. Implicit feedback for inferring user preference: a bibliography. *SIGIR Forum*, 37(2):18–28, 2003. DOI: 10.1145/959258.959260

[10] Hui Fang and ChengXiang Zhai. Web search relevance feedback. In *Encyclopedia of Database Systems*. Springer, 2009.

[11] Steuard Jensen. An introduction to lagrange multipliers, 2004. http://www.slimy.com/~steuard/teaching/tutorials/Lagrange.html.

[12] Roni Rosenfeld. Two decades of statistical language modeling: where do we go from here? In *Proceedings of IEEE*, volume 88, 2000. DOI: 10.1109/5.880083

[13] Christopher D. Manning and Hinrich Schütze. *Foundations of Statistical Natural Language Processing*. The MIT Press, Cambridge, MA, 1999.

[14] F. Jelinek. *Statistical methods for speech recognition*. MIT Press, 1997.

[15] Mandar Mitra, Chris Buckley, Amit Singhal, and Claire Cardie. An analysis of statistical and syntactic phrases. In *Proceedings of RIAO 1997*, pages 200–214, 1997.

[16] Peter F. Brown, John Cocke, Stephen A. Della Pietra, Vincent J. Della Pietra, Fredrick Jelinek, John D. Lafferty, Robert L. Mercer, and Paul S. Roossin. A statistical approach to machine translation. *Computational Linguistics*, 16(2):79–85, 1990.

[17] ChengXiang Zhai. Statistical language models for information retrieval: A critical review. *Foundations and Trends in Information Retrieval*. 2(3):137–215, 2008.

[18] R. Baeza-Yates and B. Ribeiro-Neto. *Modern Information Retrieval*. Addison-Wesley Pub. Co., 1999.

[19] C. Manning, P. Raghavan, and H. Schutze. *Introduction to Information Retrieval*. Cambridge University Press, 2008.

[20] W. B. Croft, D. Metzler, and T. D. Strohman. *Search Engines: Information Retrieval in Practice*. Pearson Education, 2009.

[21] D. Grossman and O. Frieder. *Information Retrieval: Algorithms and Heuristics*. Springer, 2004.

[22] Larry Wasserman. *All of Statistics: A Concise Course in Statistical Inference*. Springer, February 2004.

[23] G. Salton, A. Wong, and C. S. Yang. A vector space model for automatic indexing. *Communications of the ACM*, 18(11):613–620, 1975. DOI: 10.1145/361219.361220

[24] G. Salton and M. McGill. *Introduction to Modern Information Retrieval*. McGraw-Hill, 1983.

[25] G. Salton. *Automatic Text Processing: The Transformation, Analysis and Retrieval of Information by Computer*. Addison-Wesley, 1989.

[26] Amit Singhal. Modern information retrieval: A brief overview. *Bulletin of the IEEE Computer Society Technical Committee on Data Engineering*, 24(4):35–43, 2001.

[27] Karen Sparck Jones. A statistical interpretation of term specifity and its application in retrieval. *Journal of Documentation*, 28(1):11–22, 1972. DOI: 10.1108/eb026526

[28] Hui Fang, Tao Tao, and ChengXiang Zhai. A formal study of information retrieval heuristics. In *Proceedings of the 2004 ACM SIGIR Conference on Research and Development in Information Retrieval*, pp. 49–56, 2004. DOI: 10.1145/1008992.1009004

[29] S. P. Harter. A probabilistic approach to automatic keyword indexing (part I & II). *Journal of the American Society for Information Science*, 26:197–206 (Part I), 280–289 (Part II), July-August 1975.

[30] A. Bookstein and D. Swanson. A decision theoretic foundation for indexing. *Journal of the American Society for Information Science*, 26:45–50, 1975. DOI: 10.1002/asi.4630260107

[31] S. Deerwester, S. Dumais, T. Landauer, G. Furnas, and R. Harshman. Indexing by latent semantic analysis. *Journal of the American Society for Information Science*, 41:391–407, 1990. DOI: 10.1002/(SICI)1097-4571(199009)41:6<391::AID-ASI1>3.0.CO;2-9

[32] T. Hofmann. Probabilistic latent semantic indexing. In *Proceedings of ACM SIGIR'99*, pp. 50–57, 1999. DOI: 10.1145/312624.312649

[33] S. K. M. Wong and Y. Y. Yao. A probability distribution model for information retrieval. *Information Processing and Management*, 25(1):39–53, 1989. DOI: 10.1016/0306-4573(89)90090-3

[34] J. Rocchio. Relevance feedback in information retrieval. In *The SMART Retrieval System: Experiments in Automatic Document Processing*, pp. 313–323. Prentice-Hall Inc., 1971.

[35] G. Salton and C. Buckley. Improving retrieval performance by relevance feedback. *Journal of the American Society for Information Science*, 44(4):288–297, 1990. DOI: 10.1002/(SICI)1097-4571(199006)41:4<288::AID-ASI8>3.0.CO;2-H

[36] E. Fox. *Expending the Boolean and Vector Space Models of Information Retrieval with P-Norm Queries and Multiple Concept Types*. Ph.D. thesis, Cornell University, 1983.

[37] G. Salton, E. Fox, and H. Wu. Extended boolean information retrieval. *The Communications of the ACM*, 26(1):1022–1036, 1983. DOI: 10.1145/182.358466

[38] R. Rousseau. Extended Boolean retrieval: a heuristic approach. In *Proceedings of SIGIR'90*, pp. 495–508, 1990. DOI: 10.1145/96749.98255

[39] David D. Lewis. Representation and learning in information retrieval. Technical Report 91-93, University of Massachusetts, 1992.

[40] David A. Evans and ChengXiang Zhai. Noun-phrase analysis in unrestricted text for information retrieval. In *Proceedings of ACL 1996*, pp. 17–24, 1996. DOI: 10.3115/981863.981866

[41] Tomek Strzalkowski. NLP track at TREC-5. In D. Harman, editor, *Proceedings of the Fifth Text REtrieval Conference (TREC-5)*, pp. 97–102, 1997.

[42] ChengXiang Zhai. Fast statistical parsing of noun phrases for document indexing. In *5th Conference on Applied Natural Language Processing (ANLP-97)*, pp. 312–319, March 31 – April 3 1997. DOI: 10.3115/974557.974603

[43] Wessel Kraaij. *Variations on Language Modeling for Information Retrieval*. Ph.D. thesis, University of Twente, 2004. No.04-62 ISSN 1381-3617, ISBN 90-75296-09-6.

[44] Renée Pohlmann and Wessel Kraaij. The effect of syntactic phrase indexing on retrieval performance for Dutch texts. In L. Devroye and C. Chrisment, editors, *Proceedings of RIAO'97*, pp. 176–187, 1997.

[45] G. Salton and C. Buckley. Term-weighting approaches in automatic text retrieval. *Information Processing and Management*, 24:513–523, 1988. DOI: 10.1016/0306-4573(88)90021-0

[46] A. Singhal, C. Buckley, and M. Mitra. Pivoted document length normalization. In *Proceedings of the 1996 ACM SIGIR Conference on Research and Development in Information Retrieval*, pp. 21–29, 1996. DOI: 10.1145/243199.243206

[47] G. Salton, C. S. Yang, and C. T. Yu. A theory of term importance in automatic text analysis. *Journal of the American Society for Information Science*, 26(1):33–44, Jan.-Feb. 1975. DOI: 10.1002/asi.4630260106

[48] Gianni Amati and Cornelis Joost Van Rijsbergen. Probabilistic models of information retrieval based on measuring the divergence from randomness. *ACM Transactions on Information Systems*, 20(4):357–389, 2002. DOI: 10.1145/582415.582416

[49] Karen Sparck Jones, Steve Walker, and Stephen E. Robertson. A probabilistic model of information retrieval: development and comparative experiments - part 1 and part 2. *Information Processing and Management*, 36(6):779–808 and 809–840, 2000.

[50] S. E. Robertson. The probability ranking principle in IR. *Journal of Documentation*, 33(4):294–304, Dec. 1977. DOI: 10.1108/eb026647

[51] N. Fuhr and C. Buckley. A probabilistic learning approach for document indexing. *ACM Transactions on Information Systems*, 9(3):223–248, 1991. DOI: 10.1145/125187.125189

[52] F. Gey. Inferring probability of relevance using the method of logistic regression. In *Proceedings of ACM SIGIR'94*, pp. 222–231, 1994.

[53] Thorsten Joachims, Hang Li, Tie-Yan Liu, and ChengXiang Zhai. *Proceedings of ACM SIGIR 2007 Workshop on Learning to Rank for Information Retrieval*. 2007. http://research.microsoft.com/users/LR4IR-2007/.

[54] Donald Metzler and W. Bruce Croft. A Markov random field model for term dependencies. In *Proceedings of the 2005 ACM SIGIR Conference on Research and Development in Information Retrieval*, pp. 472–479, 2005. DOI: 10.1145/1076034.1076115

[55] John Lafferty and ChengXiang Zhai. Probabilistic relevance models based on document and query generation. In W. Bruce Croft and John Lafferty, editors, *Language Modeling and Information Retrieval*, pp. 1–6. Kluwer Academic Publishers, 2003.

[56] S. Robertson and K. Sparck Jones. Relevance weighting of search terms. *Journal of the American Society for Information Science*, 27:129–146, 1976. DOI: 10.1002/asi.4630270302

[57] C. J. van Rijsbergen. *Information Retrieval*. Butterworths, 1979.

[58] N. Fuhr. Probabilistic models in information retrieval. *The Computer Journal*, 35(3):243–255, 1992. DOI: 10.1093/comjnl/35.3.243

[59] David D. Lewis. Naive (Bayes) at forty: The independence assumption in information retrieval. In *European Conference on Machine Learning*, pp. 4–15, 1998. DOI: 10.1007/BFb0026666

[60] W. Cooper. Some inconsistencies and misnomers in probabilistic IR. In *Proceedings of SIGIR'91*, pp. 57–61, 1991. DOI: 10.1145/122860.122866

[61] C. J. van Rijbergen. A theoretical basis for the use of co-occurrence data in information retrieval. *Journal of Documentation*, pp. 106–119, 1977. DOI: 10.1108/eb026637

[62] D. J. Harper and C. J. van Rijsbergen. An evaluation of feedback in document retrieval using co-occurrence data. *Journal of Documentation*, 34(3):189–216, 1978. DOI: 10.1108/eb026659

[63] W. B. Croft. Document representation in probabilistic models of information retrieval. *Journal of the American Society for Information Science*, pp. 451–457, Nov. 1981. DOI: 10.1002/asi.4630320609

[64] S. E. Robertson, C. J. van Rijsbergen, and M. F. Porter. Probabilistic models of indexing and searching. In R. N. Oddy et al., editors, *Information Retrieval Research*, pp. 35–56. Butterworths, 1981.

[65] Thomas Kalt. A new probabilistic model of text classification and retrieval. Technical Report 78, CIIR, University of Massachusetts, 1996.

[66] Andrew McCallum and Kamal Nigam. A comparison of event models for Naive Bayes text classification. In *AAAI-1998 Learning for Text Categorization Workshop*, pp. 41–48, 1998.

[67] S. Robertson and K. Sparck Jones. Simple, proven approaches to text retrieval. Technical report, University of Cambridge, 1994. UCAM-CL-TR-356.

[68] W. B. Croft and D. J. Harper. Using probabilistic models of document retrieval without relevance information. *Journal of Documentation*, 35:285–295, 1979. DOI: 10.1108/eb026683

[69] S. Robertson and S. Walker. On relevance weights with little relevance information. In *Proceedings of SIGIR'97*, pp. 16–24, 1997. DOI: 10.1145/258525.258529

[70] S. E. Robertson and S. Walker. Some simple effective approximations to the 2-Poisson model for probabilistic weighted retrieval. In *Proceedings of SIGIR'94*, pp. 232–241, 1994.

[71] Victor Lavrenko and W. Bruce Croft. Relevance-based language models. In *Proceedings of SIGIR'01*, pp. 120–127, Sept. 2001. DOI: 10.1145/383952.383972

[72] M. E. Maron and J. L. Kuhns. On relevance, probabilistic indexing and information retrieval. *Journal of the ACM*, 7:216–244, 1960. DOI: 10.1145/321033.321035

[73] John Lafferty and ChengXiang Zhai. Probabilistic IR models based on query and document generation. In *Proceedings of the Language Modeling and IR Workshop*, pp. 1–5, May 31 – June 1, 2001.

[74] J. Ponte and W. B. Croft. A language modeling approach to information retrieval. In *Proceedings of the ACM SIGIR'98*, pp. 275–281, 1998. DOI: 10.1145/290941.291008

[75] D. Hiemstra and W. Kraaij. Twenty-One at TREC-7: Ad-hoc and cross-language track. In *Proceedings of Seventh Text REtrieval Conference (TREC-7)*, pp. 227–238, 1998.

[76] D. H. Miller, T. Leek, and R. Schwartz. A hidden Markov model information retrieval system. In *Proceedings of the 1999 ACM SIGIR Conference on Research and Development in Information Retrieval*, pp. 214–221, 1999. DOI: 10.1145/312624.312680

[77] Elke Mittendorf and Peter Schauble. Document and passage retrieval based on hidden Markov models. In *Proceedings of SIGIR'94*, pp. 318–327, 1994.

[78] C. J. van Rijsbergen. A non-classical logic for information retrieval. *The Computer Journal*, 29(6), pp. 481–485, 1986. DOI: 10.1093/comjnl/29.6.481

[79] S. K. M. Wong and Y. Y. Yao. On modeling information retrieval with probabilistic inference. *ACM Transactions on Information Systems*, 13(1):69–99, 1995. DOI: 10.1145/195705.195713

[80] Norbert Fuhr. Language models and uncertain inference in information retrieval. In *Proceedings of the Language Modeling and IR Workshop*, pp. 6–11, May 31 – June 1 2001.

[81] Howard Turtle and W. Bruce Croft. Evaluation of an inference network-based retrieval model. *ACM Transactions on Information Systems*, 9(3):187–222, 1991. DOI: 10.1145/125187.125188

[82] R. Fung and B. Del Favero. Applying Bayesian networks to information retrieval. *Communications of the ACM*, 38(3):42–48, 1995. DOI: 10.1145/203330.203340

[83] Berthier A. N. Ribeiro and Richard Muntz. A belief network model for IR. In *Proceedings of SIGIR'96*, pp. 253–260, 1996. DOI: 10.1145/243199.243272

[84] B. Ribeiro-Neto, I. Silva, and R. Muntz. Bayesian network models for information retrieval. In F. Crestani and G. Pasi, editors, *Soft Computing in Information Retrieval: Techniques and Applications*, pp. 259–291. Springer-Verlag, 2000.

[85] J. P. Callan, W.B. Croft, and S.M. Harding. The inquery retrieval system. In *Proceedings of the Third International Conference on Database and Expert System Applications*, pp. 78–82. Springer-Verlag, 1992.

[86] K. L. Kwok. A network approach to probabilistic information retrieval. *ACM Transactions on Office Information System*, 13:324–353, 1995. DOI: 10.1145/203052.203067

[87] Hui Fang and ChengXiang Zhai. An exploration of axiomatic approach to information retrieval. In *Proceedings of ACM SIGIR 2005*, 2005. DOI: 10.1145/1076034.1076116

[88] Hui Fang and ChengXiang Zhai. Semantic term matching in axiomatic approaches to information retrieval. In Efthimis N. Efthimiadis, Susan T. Dumais, David Hawking, and Kalervo Järvelin, editors, *Proceedings of SIGIR 2006*, pp. 115–122. ACM, 2006. DOI: 10.1145/1148170.1148193

[89] C. Zhai. *Risk Minimization and Language Modeling in Text Retrieval*. Ph.D. thesis, Carnegie Mellon University, 2002. DOI: 10.1145/792550.792571

[90] ChengXiang Zhai and John Lafferty. A risk minimization framework for information retrieval. *Information Processing and Management*, 42(1):31–55, 2006. DOI: 10.1016/j.ipm.2004.11.003

[91] ChengXiang Zhai, William W. Cohen, and John Lafferty. Beyond independent relevance: Methods and evaluation metrics for subtopic retrieval. In *Proceedings of ACM SIGIR'03*, pp. 10–17, Aug. 2003. DOI: 10.1145/860435.860440

[92] V. Lavrenko. *A Generative Theory of Relevance*. Ph.D. thesis, University of Massachusetts, Amherst, 2004.

[93] W. S. Cooper and M. E. Maron. Foundations of probabilistic and utility-theoretic indexing. *Journal of the ACM*, 25(1):67–80, 1978. DOI: 10.1145/322047.322053

[94] ChengXiang Zhai and John Lafferty. A study of smoothing methods for language models applied to ad hoc information retrieval. In *Proceedings of ACM SIGIR'01*, pp. 334–342, Sept 2001. DOI: 10.1145/383952.384019

[95] Qiaozhu Mei, Hui Fang, and ChengXiang Zhai. A study of Poisson query generation model for information retrieval. In *Proceedings of the 30th Annual International ACM SIGIR Conference on Research and Development in Information Retrieval*, pp. 319–326, 2007. DOI: 10.1145/1277741.1277797

[96] Donald Metzler, Victor Lavrenko, and W. Bruce Croft. Formal multiple-Bernoulli models for language modeling. In *SIGIR '04: Proceedings of the 27th Annual international ACM SIGIR conference on Research and Development in Information Retrieval*, pp. 540–541, New York, ACM, 2004. DOI: 10.1145/1008992.1009110

[97] F. Song and W. B. Croft. A general language model for information retrieval. In *Proceedings of the 1999 ACM SIGIR Conference on Research and Development in Information Retrieval*, pp. 279–280, 1999. DOI: 10.1145/312624.312698

[98] ChengXiang Zhai and John Lafferty. A study of smoothing methods for language models applied to information retrieval. *ACM Transactions on Information Systems*, 2(2):179–214, 2004. DOI: 10.1145/984321.984322

[99] S. F. Chen and J. Goodman. An empirical study of smoothing techniques for language modeling. Technical Report TR-10-98, Harvard University, 1998. DOI: 10.1006/csla.1999.0128

[100] Djoerd Hiemstra. *Using Language Models for Information Retrieval*. Ph.D. thesis, University of Twente, 2001. ISSN 1381-3617 (no. 01-32), ISBN 90-75296-05-3.

[101] H. Ney, U. Essen, and R. Kneser. On structuring probabilistic dependencies in stochastic language modeling. *Computer Speech and Language*, 8:1–38, 1994. DOI: 10.1006/csla.1994.1001

[102] S. M. Katz. Estimation of probabilities from sparse data for the language model component of a speech recognizer. *IEEE Transactions on Acoustics, Speech and Signal Processing*, ASSP-35:400–401, 1987. DOI: 10.1109/TASSP.1987.1165125

[103] I. J. Good. The population frequencies of species and the estimation of population parameters. *Biometrika*, 40, parts 3,4:237–264, 1953. DOI: 10.1093/biomet/40.3-4.237

[104] William Gale. Good turing smoothing without tears. Statistics Reports from AT&T Laboratories 94.5, AT&T Bell Laboratories, 1994.

[105] Djoerd Hiemstra. A probabilistic justification for using tf x idf term weighting in information retrieval. *International Journal on Digital Libraries*, 3(2):131–139, 2000.

[106] Oren Kurland and Lillian Lee. Corpus structure, language models, and ad hoc information retrieval. In *SIGIR '04: Proceedings of the 27th Annual International Conference on Research and Development in Information Retrieval*, pp. 194–201. ACM Press, 2004. DOI: 10.1145/1008992.1009027

[107] Xiaoyong Liu and W. Bruce Croft. Cluster-based retrieval using language models. In *SIGIR '04: Proceedings of the 27th Annual International Conference on Research and Development in Information Retrieval*, pp. 186–193. ACM Press, 2004. DOI: 10.1145/1008992.1009026

[108] Azadeh Shakery and ChengXiang Zhai. Smoothing document language models with probabilistic term count propagation. *Information Retrieval*, 11(2):139–164, 2008. DOI: 10.1007/s10791-007-9041-9

[109] ChengXiang Zhai and John Lafferty. Two-stage language models for information retrieval. In *Proceedings of ACM SIGIR'02*, pp. 49–56, Aug. 2002. DOI: 10.1145/564376.564387

[110] A. Berger and J. Lafferty. Information retrieval as statistical translation. In *Proceedings of the 1999 ACM SIGIR Conference on Research and Development in Information Retrieval*, pp. 222–229, 1999. DOI: 10.1145/312624.312681

[111] W. Kraaij, T. Westerveld, and D. Hiemstra. The importance of prior probabilities for entry page search. In *Proceedings of ACM SIGIR 2002*, pp. 27–34, 2002. DOI: 10.1145/564376.564383

[112] Xiaoyan Li and W. Bruce Croft. Time-based language models. In *CIKM '03: Proceedings of the Twelfth International Conference on Information and Knowledge Management*, pp. 469–475, New York, ACM, 2003. DOI: 10.1145/956863.956951

[113] Oren Kurland and Lillian Lee. Pagerank without hyperlinks: structural re-ranking using links induced by language models. In *SIGIR '05: Proceedings of the 28th Annual International ACM SIGIR Conference on Research and Development in Information Retrieval*, pp. 306–313, New York, ACM, 2005. DOI: 10.1145/1076034.1076087

[114] Yun Zhou and W. Bruce Croft. Document quality models for web ad hoc retrieval. In *CIKM '05: Proceedings of the 14th ACM International Conference on Information and Knowledge Management*, pp. 331–332, New York, ACM, 2005. DOI: 10.1145/1099554.1099652

[115] Xiaoyong Liu and W. Bruce Croft. Passage retrieval based on language models. In *CIKM '02: Proceedings of the Eleventh International Conference on Information and Knowledge Management*, pp. 375–382, New York, ACM, 2002. DOI: 10.1145/584792.584854

[116] P. Ogilvie and J. Callan. Experiments using the Lemur toolkit. In *Proceedings of the 2001 TREC Conference*, 2002.

[117] ChengXiang Zhai, Tao Tao, Hui Fang, and Zhidi Shang. Improving the robustness of language models - UIUC TREC 2003 robust and genomics experiments. In *TREC*, pp. 667–672, 2003.

[118] Xing Wei and W. Bruce Croft. LDA-based document models for ad-hoc retrieval. In *SIGIR '06: Proceedings of the 29th Annual International ACM SIGIR Conference on Research and Development in Information Retrieval*, pp. 178–185, New York, ACM, 2006. DOI: 10.1145/1148170.1148204

[119] Amit Singhal and Fernando Pereira. Document expansion for speech retrieval. In *SIGIR '99: Proceedings of the 22nd Annual International ACM SIGIR Conference on Research and Development in Information Retrieval*, pp. 34–41, New York, ACM, 1999. DOI: 10.1145/312624.312645

[120] Victor Lavrenko, James Allan, Edward DeGuzman, Daniel LaFlamme, Veera Pollard, and Stephen Thomas. Relevance models for topic detection and tracking. In *Proceedings of the Second International Conference on Human Language Technology Research*, pp. 115–121, San Francisco, CA, 2002. Morgan Kaufmann Publishers Inc.

[121] Ramesh Nallapati and James Allan. Capturing term dependencies using a language model based on sentence trees. In *CIKM '02: Proceedings of the Eleventh International Conference on Information and Knowledge Management*, pp. 383–390, New York, ACM, 2002. DOI: 10.1145/584792.584855

[122] Munirathnam Srikanth and Rohini Srihari. Exploiting syntactic structure of queries in a language modeling approach to IR. In *CIKM '03: Proceedings of the Twelfth International Conference on Information and Knowledge Management*, pp. 476–483, New York, NY, ACM, 2003. DOI: 10.1145/956863.956952

[123] Jianfeng Gao, Jian-Yun Nie, Guangyuan Wu, and Guihong Cao. Dependence language model for information retrieval. In *SIGIR '04: Proceedings of the 27th Annual International ACM SIGIR Conference on Research and Development in Information Retrieval*, pp. 170–177, New York, ACM, 2004. DOI: 10.1145/1008992.1009024

[124] Tomek Strzalkowski and Barbara Vauthey. Information retrieval using robust natural language processing. In *Proceedings of the 30th Annual Meeting on Association for Computational Linguistics*, pp. 104–111, Morristown, NJ, 1992. Association for Computational Linguistics. DOI: 10.3115/981967.981981

[125] Djoerd Hiemstra, Stephen Robertson, and Hugo Zaragoza. Parsimonious language models for information retrieval. In *SIGIR '04: Proceedings of the 27th Annual International ACM SIGIR Conference on Research and Development in Information Retrieval*, pp. 178–185, New York, ACM, 2004. DOI: 10.1145/1008992.1009025

[126] Hugo Zaragoza, Djoerd Hiemstra, and Michael E. Tipping. Bayesian extension to the language model for ad hoc information retrieval. In *Proceedings of ACM SIGIR 2003*, pp. 4–9, 2003. DOI: 10.1145/860435.860439

[127] Rong Jin, Alexander G. Hauptmann, and ChengXiang Zhai. Title language model for information retrieval. In *Proceedings of ACM SIGIR 2002*, pp. 42–48, 2002. DOI: 10.1145/564376.564386

[128] Guihong Cao, Jian-Yun Nie, and Jing Bai. Integrating word relationships into language models. In *Proceedings of the 2005 ACM SIGIR Conference on Research and Development in Information Retrieval*, pp. 298–305, 2005. DOI: 10.1145/1076034.1076039

[129] Adam L. Berger and John D. Lafferty. The Weaver system for document retrieval. In *Proceedings of TREC 1999*, 1999.

[130] Jinxi Xu, Ralph Weischedel, and Chanh Nguyen. Evaluating a probabilistic model for cross-lingual information retrieval. In *SIGIR '01: Proceedings of the 24th Annual International ACM SIGIR Conference on Research and Development in Information Retrieval*, pp. 105–110, New York, NY, ACM, 2001. DOI: 10.1145/383952.383968

[131] J. Ponte. *A Language Modeling Approach to Information Retrieval*. Ph.D. thesis, University of Massachusetts at Amherst, 1998. DOI: 10.1145/290941.291008

[132] Kenney Ng. A maximum likelihood ratio information retrieval model. In E. Voorhees and D. Harman, editors, *Proceedings of the Eighth Text REtrieval Conference (TREC-8)*, pp. 483–492, 2000.

[133] Djoerd Hiemstra. Term-specific smoothing for the language modeling approach to information retrieval: the importance of a query term. In *Proceedings of ACM SIGIR 2002*, pp. 35–41, 2002. DOI: 10.1145/564376.564385

[134] ChengXiang Zhai and John Lafferty. Model-based feedback in the language modeling approach to information retrieval. In *Proceedings of the Tenth International Conference on Information and Knowledge Management (CIKM 2001)*, pp. 403–410, 2001.

[135] J. Xu and W. B. Croft. Cluster-based language models for distributed retrieval. In *Proceedings of ACM SIGIR'99*, pp. 254–261, 1999. DOI: 10.1016/S0165-1684(98)00188-1

[136] Jianhua Lin. Divergence measures based on the shannon entropy. *IEEE Transactions on Information Theory*, 37(1):145–151, 1991. DOI: 10.1109/18.61115

[137] Hui Fang, Tao Tao, and ChengXiang Zhai. An exploration of formalized retrieval heuristics. In *Proceedings of the ACM SIGIR'03 Workshop on Mathematical/Formal Methods in Information Retrieval*, Aug. 2003.

[138] Xuanhui Wang, Hui Fang, and ChengXiang Zhai. Improve retrieval accuracy for difficult queries using negative feedback. In *CIKM '07: Proceedings of the Sixteenth ACM Conference on Conference on Information and Knowledge Management*, pp. 991–994, New York, ACM, 2007. DOI: 10.1145/1321440.1321593

[139] Tao Tao and ChengXiang Zhai. Regularized estimation of mixture models for robust pseudo-relevance feedback. In *Proceedings of ACM SIGIR 2006*, pp. 162–169, 2006. DOI: 10.1145/1148170.1148201

[140] A. P. Dempster, N. M. Laird, and D. B. Rubin. Maximum likelihood from incomplete data via the EM algorithm. *Journal of Royal Statistics Society B*, 39:1–38, 1977.

[141] ChengXiang Zhai. A note on expectation-maximization (EM) algorithm, 2007. `http://sifaka.cs.uiuc.edu/czhai/pub/em-note.pdf`.

[142] Tao Tao and ChengXiang Zhai. Mixture clustering model for pseudo feedback in information retrieval. In *Proceedings of the 2004 Meeting of the International Federation of Classification Societies*. Springer, 2004.

[143] Kevyn Collins-Thompson and Jamie Callan. Estimation and use of uncertainty in pseudo-relevance feedback. In *Proceedings of ACM SIGIR 2007*, pp. 303–310, 2007.

[144] Lawrence Page, Sergey Brin, Rajeev Motwani, and Terry Winograd. The pagerank citation ranking: Bringing order to the web. Technical report, Stanford Digital Library Technologies Project, 1998.

[145] J. Xu and W. B. Croft. Query expansion using local and global document analysis. In *Proceedings of the SIGIR'96*, pp. 4–11, 1996. DOI: 10.1016/0165-1684(96)00012-6

[146] Kevyn Collins-Thompson and Jamie Callan. Query expansion using random walk models. In *Proceedings of ACM CIKM 2005*, pp. 704–711, 2005. DOI: 10.1145/1099554.1099727

[147] Victor Lavrenko, Martin Choquette, and W. Bruce Croft. Cross-lingual relevance models. In *Proceedings of SIGIR 2002*, pp. 175–182, 2002. DOI: 10.1145/564376.564408

[148] Jing Bai, Jian-Yun Nie, Guihong Cao, and Hugues Bouchard. Using query contexts in information retrieval. In *Proceedings of ACM SIGIR 2007*, pp. 15–22, 2007. DOI: 10.1145/1277741.1277747

[149] William R. Hersh et al. TREC 2003 genomics track overview, *Proceedings of TREC 2003*, 2003.

[150] V. Lavrenko, X. Yi, and J. Allan. Information retrieval on empty fields. In *Proceedings of NAACL-HLT 2007*, pp. 89–96, 2007.

[151] Xuanhui Wang, Hui Fang, and ChengXiang Zhai. A study of methods for negative relevance feedback. In Sung-Hyon Myaeng, Douglas W. Oard, Fabrizio Sebastiani, Tat-Seng Chua, and Mun-Kew Leong, editors, *Proceedings of SIGIR 2008*, pp. 219–226. ACM, 2008. DOI: 10.1145/1390334.1390374

[152] Yi Zhang and James P. Callan. The bias problem and language models in adaptive filtering. In *Proceedings of TREC 2001*, 2001.

[153] Hubert Jin, Rich Schwartz, Sreenivasa Sista, and Frederick Walls. Topic tracking for radio, tv broadcast, and newswire. In *Proceedings of the DARPA Broadcast News Workshop*, pp. 199–204, 1999.

[154] M. Spitters and W. Kraaij. Language models for topic tracking. In *Language Modeling for Information Retrieval*, pp. 95–124, 2003.

[155] Christopher M. Bishop. *Pattern Recognition and Machine Learning*. Springer, 2006. DOI: 10.1117/1.2819119

[156] Djoerd Hiemstra and Franciska de Jong. Disambiguation strategies for cross-language information retrieval. In Serge Abiteboul and Anne-Marie Vercoustre, editors, *ECDL*, volume 1696 of *Lecture Notes in Computer Science*, pp. 274–293. Springer, 1999. DOI: 10.1007/3-540-48155-9_18

[157] Luo Si, Rong Jin, James P. Callan, and Paul Ogilvie. A language modeling framework for resource selection and results merging. In *Proceedings of CIKM 2002*, pp. 391–397, 2002. DOI: 10.1145/584792.584856

[158] J. Callan. Distributed information retrieval. In W. B. Croft, editor, *Advances in Information Retrieval*, pp. 127–150. Kluwer Academic Publishers, 2000. DOI: 10.1007/0-306-47019-5_5

[159] Paul Ogilvie and James P. Callan. Combining document representations for known-item search. In *Proceedings of SIGIR 2003*, pp. 143–150, 2003. DOI: 10.1145/860435.860463

[160] Djoerd Hiemstra. Statistical language models for intelligent XML retrieval. In *Intelligent Search on XML Data*, pp. 107–118, 2003. DOI: 10.1007/b13249

[161] Azadeh Shakery and ChengXiang Zhai. A probabilistic relevance propagation model for hypertext retrieval. In *Proceedings of CIKM 2006*, pp. 550–558, 2006. DOI: 10.1145/1183614.1183693

[162] Tao Qin, Tie-Yan Liu, Xu-Dong Zhang, Zheng Chen, and Wei-Ying Ma. A study of relevance propagation for web search. In *Proceedings of SIGIR 2005*, pp. 408–415, 2005. DOI: 10.1145/1076034.1076105

[163] Xuehua Shen, Bin Tan, and ChengXiang Zhai. Privacy protection in personalized search. *SIGIR Forum*, 41(1):4–17, 2007. DOI: 10.1145/1273221.1273222

[164] Xuehua Shen, Bin Tan, and ChengXiang Zhai. Context-sensitive information retrieval using implicit feedback. In *Proceedings of SIGIR 2005*, pp. 43–50, 2005. DOI: 10.1145/1076034.1076045

[165] Bin Tan, Xuehua Shen, and ChengXiang Zhai. Mining long-term search history to improve search accuracy. In *Proceedings of KDD 2006*, pp. 718–723, 2006. DOI: 10.1145/1150402.1150493

[166] Bin Tan, Atulya Velivelli, Hui Fang, and ChengXiang Zhai. Term feedback for information retrieval with language models. In Wessel Kraaij, Arjen P. de Vries, Charles L. A. Clarke, Norbert Fuhr, and Noriko Kando, editors, *Proceedings of SIGIR 2007*, pp. 263–270. ACM, 2007. DOI: 10.1145/1277741.1277788

[167] H. Fang and C. Zhai. Probabilistic models for expert finding. In *Proceedings of ECIR 2007*, pp. 418–430, 2007. DOI: 10.1007/978-3-540-71496-5_38

[168] Krisztian Balog, Leif Azzopardi, and Maarten de Rijke. Formal models for expert finding in enterprise corpora. In *Proceedings of SIGIR-06*, pp. 43–50, 2006. DOI: 10.1145/1148170.1148181

[169] Jing Jiang and ChengXiang Zhai. Extraction of coherent relevant passages using hidden markov models. *ACM Transactions on Information Systems*, 24(3):295–319, 2006. DOI: 10.1145/1165774.1165775

[170] L. R. Rabiner. A tutorial on hidden Markov models. In *Proceedings of the IEEE*, 77(2):257–285, 1989. DOI: 10.1109/5.18626

[171] Jaime Carbonell and Jade Goldstein. The use of MMR, diversity-based reranking for reordering documents and producing summaries. In *Proceedings of SIGIR'98*, pp. 335–336, 1998. DOI: 10.1145/290941.291025

[172] D. Blei, A. Ng, and M. Jordan. Latent Dirichlet allocation. *Journal of Machine Learning Research*, 3:993–1022, 2003. DOI: 10.1162/jmlr.2003.3.4-5.993

[173] M. Karimzadehgan, C. Zhai, and G. Belford. Multi-aspect expertise matching for review assignment. In *Proceedings of the 17th ACM International Conference on Information and Knowledge Management*, pp. 1113-1122, 2008.

[174] James Allan, Jaime Carbonell, George Doddington, Jonathan Yamron, Yiming Yang, James Allan Umass, Brian Archibald Cmu, Doug Beeferman Cmu, Adam Berger Cmu, Ralf Brown Cmu, Ira Carp Dragon, George Doddington Darpa, Alex Hauptmann Cmu, John Lafferty Cmu, Victor Lavrenko Umass, Ron Papka Umass, Jay Ponte Umass, and Mike Scudder Umass. Topic detection and tracking pilot study: Final report. In *Proceedings of the DARPA Broadcast News Transcription and Understanding Workshop*, pp. 194–218, 1998.

[175] J. Allan, H. Jin, M. Rajman, C. Wayne, D. Gildea, V. Lavrenko, R. Hoberman, and D. Caputo. Topic-based novelty detection: 1999 summer workshop at clsp, 1999. final report. Available at http://www.clsp.jhu.edu/ws99/tdt.

[176] Yi Zhang, Jamie Callan, and Thomas Minka. Redundancy detection in adaptive filtering. In *Proceedings of SIGIR'02*, pp. 81–88, Aug. 2002. DOI: 10.1145/564376.564393

[177] Steve Cronen-Townsend, Yun Zhou, and W. Bruce Croft. Predicting query performance. In *Proceedings of the 25th Annual International ACM SIGIR Conference on Research and Development in Information Retrieval (SIGIR 2002)*, pp. 299–306, Aug. 2002. DOI: 10.1145/564376.564429

[178] T. Hofmann. Probabilistic latent semantic analysis. In *Proceedings of UAI 1999*, pp. 289–296, 1999.

[179] G. J. McLachlan and T. Krishnan. *The EM Algorithm and Extensions*. John Wiley & Sons, Inc., 1997.

[180] Qiaozhu Mei, Xuehua Shen, and ChengXiang Zhai. Automatic labeling of multinomial topic models. In Pavel Berkhin, Rich Caruana, and Xindong Wu, editors, *Proceedings of KDD 2007*, pp. 490–499. ACM, 2007. DOI: 10.1145/1281192.1281246

[181] Xu Ling, Qiaozhu Mei, ChengXiang Zhai, and Bruce R. Schatz. Mining multi-faceted overviews of arbitrary topics in a text collection. In Ying Li, Bing Liu, and Sunita Sarawagi, editors, *Proceedings of KDD 2008*, pp. 497–505. ACM, 2008. DOI: 10.1145/1401890.1401952

[182] Thomas Hofmann. The cluster-abstraction model: Unsupervised learning of topic hierarchies from text data. In *Proceedings of IJCAI' 99*, pp. 682–687, 1999.

[183] Qiaozhu Mei and ChengXiang Zhai. A mixture model for contextual text mining. In *Proceedings of KDD '06*, pp. 649–655, 2006. DOI: 10.1145/1150402.1150482

[184] Bradley P. Carlin and Thomas A. Louis. *Bayes and Empirical Bayes Methods for Data Analysis*. Chapman & Hall/CRC, 2nd ed., 2000.

[185] Thomas Minka and John Lafferty. Expectation-propagation for the generative aspect model. In *Proceedings of the UAI 2002*, pp. 352–359, 2002.

[186] Jonathan K. Pritchard, Matthew Stephens, and Peter Donnelly. Inference of population structure using multilocus genotype data. *Genetics*, 155(2):945–959, June 2000.

[187] Thomas Griffiths. Gibbs sampling in the generative model of latent dirichlet allocation. Technical report, Stanford University, 2002. http://www-psych.stanford.edu/~gruffydd/reports/lda.ps.

[188] David M. Blei and Pedro J. Moreno. Topic segmentation with an aspect hidden markov model. In W. Bruce Croft, David J. Harper, Donald H. Kraft, and Justin Zobel, editors, *Proceedings of SIGIR 2001*, pp. 343–348. ACM, 2001. DOI: 10.1145/383952.384021

[189] Fernando C. N. Pereira, Naftali Tishby, and Lillian Lee. Distributional clustering of english words. In *Proceedings of ACL 1993*, pp. 183–190, 1993.

[190] L. Douglas Baker and Andrew McCallum. Distributional clustering of words for text classification. In *Proceedings of SIGIR 1998*, pp. 96–103. ACM, 1998. DOI: 10.3115/981574.981598

[191] ChengXiang Zhai, Atulya Velivelli, and Bei Yu. A cross-collection mixture model for comparative text minning. In *Proceeding of the 10th ACM SIGKDD International Conference on Knowledge Discovery in Data Mining*, pp. 743–748, 2004. DOI: 10.1145/1014052.1014150

[192] Mark Steyvers, Padhraic Smyth, Michal Rosen-Zvi, and Thomas Griffiths. Probabilistic author-topic models for information discovery. In *Proceedings of KDD'04*, pp. 306–315, 2004. DOI: 10.1145/1014052.1014087

[193] Qiaozhu Mei, Xu Ling, Matthew Wondra, Hang Su, and ChengXiang Zhai. Topic sentiment mixture: Modeling facets and opinions in weblogs. In *Proceedings of WWW '07*, pp. 171-180, 2007. DOI: 10.1145/1242572.1242596

[194] Qiaozhu Mei, Deng Cai, Duo Zhang, and ChengXiang Zhai. Topic modeling with network regularization. In Jinpeng Huai, Robin Chen, Hsiao-Wuen Hon, Yunhao Liu, Wei-Ying Ma, Andrew Tomkins, and Xiaodong Zhang, editors, *Proceedings of WWW 2008*, pp. 101–110. ACM, 2008. DOI: 10.1145/1367497.1367512

[195] D. Blei, T. Griffiths, M. Jordan, and J. Tenenbaum. Hierarchical topic models and the nested chinese restaurant process. In *Neural Information Processing Systems (NIPS) 16*, 2003.

[196] David M. Blei and Michael I. Jordan. Modeling annotated data. In *Proceedings of SIGIR 2003*, pp. 127–134, 2003. DOI: 10.1145/860435.860460

[197] Thomas L. Griffiths, Mark Steyvers, David M. Blei, and Joshua B. Tenenbaum. Integrating topics and syntax. In *NIPS '04: Advances in Neural Information Processing Systems 17*, 2004.

[198] David M. Blei and John D. Lafferty. Dynamic topic models. In *Proceedings of the 23rd International Conference on Machine Learning*, pp. 113–120, 2006. DOI: 10.1145/1143844.1143859

[199] Michal Rosen-Zvi, Thomas L. Griffiths, Mark Steyvers, and Padhraic Smyth. The author-topic model for authors and documents. In David Maxwell Chickering and Joseph Y. Halpern, editors, *Proceedings of UAI 2004*, pp. 487–494. AUAI Press, 2004.

[200] David Blei and John Lafferty. Correlated topic models. In *NIPS '05: Advances in Neural Information Processing Systems 18*, 2005.

[201] Wei Li and Andrew McCallum. Pachinko allocation: Dag-structured mixture models of topic correlations. In *ICML '06: Proceedings of the 23rd International Conference on Machine Learning*, pp. 577–584, 2006. DOI: 10.1145/1143844.1143917

[202] Rasmus Elsborg Madsen, David Kauchak, and Charles Elkan. Modeling word burstiness using the dirichlet distribution. In Luc De Raedt and Stefan Wrobel, editors, *Proceedings of ICML 2005*, volume 119 of *ACM International Conference Proceeding Series*, pp. 545–552. ACM, 2005. DOI: 10.1145/1102351.1102420

[203] Chris Burges, Tal Shaked, Erin Renshaw, Ari Lazier, Matt Deeds, Nicole Hamilton, and Greg Hullender. Learning to rank using gradient descent. In *ICML '05: Proceedings of the 22nd International Conference on Machine Learning*, pp. 89–96, New York, ACM, 2005. DOI: 10.1145/1102351.1102363

[204] T. Joachims. Optimizing search engines using clickthrough data. In *Proceedings of the ACM KDD 2002*, pp. 133–142, 2002. DOI: 10.1145/775047.775067

[205] Xuanhui Wang, ChengXiang Zhai, Xiao Hu, and Richard Sproat, Mining correlated bursty topic patterns from coordinated text streams, *KDD '07: Proceedings of the 13th ACM SIGKDD International Conference on Knowledge Discovery and Data Mining*, 784–793, ACM, New York, NY, 2007. DOI: 10.1145/1281192.1281276

[206] Thomas Roelleke and Jun Wang, A parallel derivation of probabilistic information retrieval models. In *SIGR '06: Proceedings of the 29th Annual International Conference on Research and Development in Information Retrieval*, 107–114, Seattle, WA, ACM, 2006. DOI: 10.1145/1148170.1148192

Printed in the United States
by Baker & Taylor Publisher Services